An Insight to Drive

By

Kathy Higgins

Dip DI, F Inst MTD

Published by Book Bubble Press

Book Bubble Press
www.bookbubblepress.com
books@bookbubblepress.com

CONTENTS

I dedicate this book to my family, who have stood by me and supported me through my journey as a driver trainer and educator, especially my husband Brian Higgins, who gets a free driving lesson every time we drive together, whether or not he wants one!

Emily Higgins, my lovely daughter who accepted mummy is not always home and sometimes has to stay overnight to attend or deliver training courses. Joan Bingham, my sister, who has helped build Insight 2 Drive from the outset.

Finally, my late father Brian Ford, who encouraged me to take the advanced driving course, which without that I would not be here now. One of his biggest lessons was not to fear the word no. Ask anyway. The above certificate was one my dad got the year I was born and is very dear to me.

Dad's Top Tip

It is far better to arrive late than not arrive at all.

Thanks also go to, in no particular order, for adding value to this book by contributing and sharing their thoughts and funny stories.

★ John Airey – Darwin, Lancashire

★ Suen Andrews – Pembrokeshire

★ Jamie and Jeniffer Barr - Liverpool

★ Lynn Barrie - Chairman of the ADINJC

★ Ian Bint - Yorkshire

★ Jackie Bradley – Liverpool

★ Nathan Carter – Liverpool

★ Colin Chown – Aigburth

★ Leanne Condliff – Crosby

★ Joan Cupit – Liverpool

★ Mick Doggett - Northern Ireland

★ Alan Drabble - Derbyshire

★ Graham Feest - Chairman of the IMTD

★ Kev and Tracey Field - Confident Driving

★ Kevin Gilfoyle – Ellesmere Port

★ Jamie, Tom, Rachel & Cameron of Grafayo

★ Diane Hall - L of a Way to Pass

★ Tom Harrington – Co Kerry, Ireland

★ Paul Jennings - Bedfordshire

★ Derek Lawton – Newton-le-Willows

★ Martin Lindsay – Llanelli

★ Andrew Love – Kettering

- ★ Margaret Masterson – Oldham
- ★ Charles Morton - Ex Registrar of the DVSA
- ★ Antonia Louise Naylor – Whitby/Ellesmere Port
- ★ David Poole – France
- ★ Sonia Poolman – Penzance
- ★ Alan Prosser – Telford
- ★ Bev Raistrick - Merseyside
- ★ Dave Robinson – Birkenhead
- ★ Maria Rossiter - Photographer
- ★ Robin Spiers - Eastbourne
- ★ David Thompson – Glasgow
- ★ David Thomson – Wishaw, Scotland
- ★ Barbara Trafford – ADI Federation
- ★ David Wright – Warrington
- ★ Mike Yeomans – Hull

Top Tip

If you are learning to drive for life and not just trying to pass a test, it will normally result in a first-time pass

Foreword

I was responsible for the Registration and Regulation of the, at the time, forty thousand plus Instructors across GB. (2006 – 2012) I regularly spoke at DVSA (DSA), National Industry conferences and local ADI associations. It was at these events I first met Kathy Higgins. She, at that time, knew me as Registrar DVSA (DSA) and signatory on her ADI Certificate.

Kathy had a thirst for knowledge, an openness with her questions and a passion for producing safe drivers using her excellent communication skills.

On my retirement as Registrar, I was invited to join The Institute of Master Tutors of Drivers where again I came across Kathy in her role of Secretary. Through The Institute I got to know Kathy on a personal level and realised just how driven and passionate she is about everything she does. She works hard and excels in her knowledge, professionalism and commitment.

It was no surprise to me that she has now written this excellent book which is clear, concise, factual and does indeed give the reader an insight into the journey of learning to drive. The tips and hints as well as the balanced views come from Kathy's years of experience and are invaluable in becoming a safe driver.

I am sure you will enjoy reading An Insight to Drive as much as I have and enjoy the road ahead - - -

Charles D Morton MInstMTD
Registrar of Approved Driving Instructors (Retired)

There are many costs to take into consideration when learning how to drive, so make sure you've got the budget in place to see it through.

Costs include:

- A provisional driving licence
- Theory test
- Professional driving lessons (the UK average is 45 hours)
- The practical driving test

This does NOT include the cost of your first car, insurance etc.

Introduction

If you have picked up this book, it's because you are about to learn how to drive, improve your driving skills, or are looking to become an instructor yourself. Did you know only 2% of the UK population go on to do any advanced driving, or become an examiner?

Good driving used to be a badge of honour among drivers. Those drivers took pride in knowing the road rules, the latest driving techniques and keeping up to date with modern driving techniques. This is generally not the case anymore and I'm on a mission to change that.

Driving isn't just what I do for a living, it's my passion, and it's important that I drive well. I'm not saying I never make a mistake, that would be silly, I make mistakes, no one is infallible. I pride myself in aiming to drive well all the time, and I want to pass my passion onto you, whether you are a learner, an early driver, an experienced driver or someone who is looking to become a driving instructor. Driving well needs to become a respected badge of honour once again.

Throughout this book, I will take you through many steps, the dos and don'ts, the hacks and top tips, all to make your experience of learning to drive and passing your test as painless as possible.
You will also find many funny stories and anecdotes throughout the book, because learning to drive isn't always plain sailing!

Farmer's Driving Test

A farmer met the driving examiner outside the local post office to start his test on his tractor. The examiner explained the test procedure and asked the farmer some questions. One question was, "Where would you find a continuous white line?" The farmer replied in his strong Irish accent "Well sir, the only place I ever saw a white line was on a football field."

The examiner realised he wasn't going to get any correct answers proceeded to the practical test.
The test area was the main street. The examiner asked the farmer to drive to the end of the street, do a u-turn, drive back to the starting point and repeat that three times. Just as the farmer was about to drive off a boy about 14 jumped on the back of the tractor. Clipboard in hand, the examiner ran up to the farmer and told him he couldn't carry a passenger as there was no seat. The farmer looked surprised "If my son isn't with me, how am I supposed to see what's behind me?"

Tom Harrington – Eire

Getting ready to lead the last leg of the
Big Learner Relay in Liverpool 2017

My Driving Journey

Let's start at the beginning, who am I, and why did I first become a driving instructor, then a driving instructor trainer to eventually starting my business, Insight 2 Drive.

It all started with a poem

I was tidying some old cupboards when I came across a poem I had written, aged ten. I must have had an inkling of being involved in road safety even then. Okay, so it's not a prize-winning piece, but I thought I would share it with you.

The Bloody Crash

The car slid and hit the sidewalk

Spun around and turned upside down

Everyone came out and started to talk

Some were slow and just stood with a frown

In a moment the injured were out

Blood was everywhere. What a horrible sight

Call an ambulance someone said with a shout

Soon, they were driven away into the night

The men came the next day

Looked at the car

And cleared all the glass away

But the blood still stained the tar.

K E Ford 1973

I passed my driving test in 1986, but I never felt quite safe driving on my own, as I was not sure what to do if something went wrong with the car. I heard that a friend of mine had been stranded with his car, so I went to night school and did a short course on car maintenance. The course gave me a massive confidence boost to know what to look for and what to do in the event of a breakdown.

I didn't start my career as a driving instructor. I arrived at the profession when I realised what I loved most about my job as a sales representative selling veterinary medicines, was the driving. My job took me all over the country, driving on roads and routes I didn't know, navigating them all without the handy satellite navigation system, or even Google Maps. More often than not I would come home complaining to my dad, telling him about yet another near miss. He advised me to take some advanced driving lessons; he claimed I could easily pass the test. Dad had thrown down the gauntlet, so I contacted my local advanced driving group, the IAM, (Institute of Advanced Motorists), now called IAM Roadsmart.

I passed the IAM test, the first time in 1995, in a Transit van.

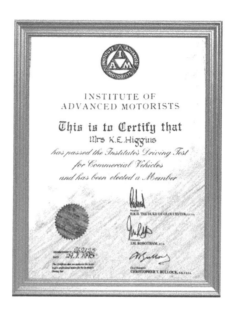

INSTITUTE OF
ADVANCED MOTORISTS

This is to Certify that
Mrs K.E. Higgins
has passed the Institute's Driving Test
for Commercial Vehicles
and has been elected a Member

H.R.H. THE DUKE OF GLOUCESTER, ...

J.M. ROBOTHAM, ...

CHRISTOPHER T. BULLOCK, ...

Training with the IAM sparked my interest in driver training and education and proved to me you can still drive well even in the 'real world'. I started my career as a driving instructor in 1995. My qualifications and CPD can be found in Appendix 1.

It was a simple decision to become an Approved Driving Instructor (ADI). I knew it would be perfect for me. I wanted to work for myself and to teach people to drive. Within two years of passing my IAM, I started my training to become a driving instructor with a National Company called Learner Driving Centres (LDC), based in Pontefract, West Yorkshire.

During my initial training, there was a sense of urgency that was growing day by day, because I was pregnant with my daughter, Emily. After failing my first attempt (part three of the ADI test), I began my career as a driving instructor, on a 'pink' training licence. After a few months I tried again and failed! I passed on my third and final attempt of the ADI test, the same week as my trainee licence was due to run out.

Driving instructors are allowed three attempts at their part two or part three tests; if they fail on the third attempt, they must wait two years from the day they passed part one of the test, before they start at part one again. They have also only got two years to pass, so the two-year countdown starts when they take and pass their part one.

I stayed with LDC for several years gaining my first ORDIT (The Official Register of Driving Instructor Trainers) registration with them, in July 2002. ORDIT is a voluntary register for people who want to train other people to become driving instructors.

LDC was the first company I worked for within the driver trainer industry and I have a lot to thank them for, especially my trainers Mike Harkin, Pat Firth and Val Wood.

I then embarked on what I can only describe as the worst episode of my career. I was advised to join a local organisation called Driving Instructor Training, based in Speke, Liverpool, not to be confused with The Driving Instructor College.

At first, working freelance for Driving Instructor Training worked well for me, I felt valued, and I could shape the training courses. During this time I also wrote a full series of workshops to support the on-road training sessions. These courses covered all parts of the driving instructor's qualification and linked them together. I introduced two other quality trainers to the establishment, and it all seemed to be going well.

Unfortunately, after about a year the company went into liquidation, and regrettably, I, along with the two trainers lost a considerable amount of money. I remain good friends with the other two instructors - you know who you are!

However, instead of letting it get me down, I saw this as a massive learning curve.

If you ever lose out, never lose the lesson.

Prof. Peter Russell MA D prof. Finst.MTD Presents Kathy Higgins with her Diploma in Driving Instruction

The First Diploma to be presented at HNC level

During this time, I met and became friends with Prof. Peter Russell, (Research Professorship and Director of the Driver Education Research Foundation (DERF) and past Chairman of the Institute of Master Tutors of Driving) who sadly passed away in 2020 with COVID-19.

Insight 2 Drive was founded in April 2007. At the outset I never wanted to be the biggest driving school, just the best. And I'm proud to say, Insight 2 Drive is now one of the most respected driving schools in the North West and is committed to not only teaching people to drive, and helping pupils not only pass their driving tests for the first time, but to drive well for life. The Insight 2 Drive team shares my passion for road safety too.

Insight 2 Drive is at the forefront of driver training, we use modern teaching methods and adapt those methods to suit the individual learner and trainee driving instructors. I and the other academy team trainers have trained most of the instructors who work as part of the Insight team. As a team we are unafraid to explore new and fun ways of teaching and training, as well as supporting all of our customers and team members.

I have now started the Insight 2 Drive Training Academy. So far, I have trained three of our driving instructors to deliver instructor training, which includes coaching instructors, helping them to run a successful ADI business and offering them ongoing support. Our instructors meet up regularly, sometimes just socially for a quick catch up and to share information and undergo continued professional development and training, this makes sure we keep educating ourselves, so we can better teach our pupils.

Insight 2 Drive doesn't just teach learner drivers. We also train and develop driving instructors and help local businesses look after their drivers, as well as offering a free service to local schools and colleges with road safety presentations for their pupils. This allows us to reach so many people and we can share our experience and knowledge to instil good driving skills for life.

I currently deliver Police Divisionary Courses, such as speed awareness for four counties. I am an NDORS trainer, which means I cascade the training down when new courses come out or are changed. In 2021 I was also appointed the Trainer Development Coach with DriveTech who are looking after the courses for Merseyside Police. I have served on the Motor Schools Association North West Committee, the Approved Driving Instructors National Joint Council. I have had close links to the Driving Instructors Association and help write the traffic light awareness course for Greater Manchester Police

Insight 2 Drive also organised and hosted three Driving Instructor Conferences in Liverpool, which were attended by instructors all over the country and I even had two delegates from Russia.

A thank you card given to me with a bottle of Vodka from Moscow

I am now the Secretary of the Institute of Master Tutors of Driving and in 2018 awarded a Fellowship of the Institute. I used to be the secretary of the Federation of Small Businesses for the Liverpool and Knowsley Branch, as you can see, I like to keep busy.

Now you know a little more about me, let's get on with my Insight to Driving and how I can help you become a better driver.

Top Tip

Give yourself a sufficient amount of time to learn how to drive and pass your test. Don't try to rush the process, as many skills are developed through experience. Taking numerous tests can be expensive, so let your instructor advise you when you are ready.

Top Tip

Record your progress

Keep yourself motivated by noting down when you've reached a big milestone and celebrate it. Some tutors use a progress log that helps pupils keep track of where they are on the syllabus, but if yours doesn't then consider making your own. There are now plenty of apps available for you to do this too.

I had a young female pupil respond very aggressively, swearing and shouting at another driver who beeped his horn when she didn't move away from the lights as quickly as he would have liked. I pulled her over in a safe place and asked her what she thought she was doing. I told her this was no way to behave and I would not tolerate it.
She said but you gave him the finger.
I said I certainly did not.
She said I saw you in the rear-view mirror
I said no, what you saw was me pointing at the L plate!!!

Joan Cupit - Liverpool

A girl on her first driving lesson got the car moving, really smoothly bringing the clutch up nicely, but then panicked and took both her hands off the wheel and covered her eyes stating,
"I am moving!"

Andrew Love – Kettering

It was raining and I was stopped at the roadside giving a brief. My learner pointed out a lady who was coming towards us, my learner said, "It looks like she might be selling something."

As the lady got closer and closer to the car, I gesticulated to say no thanks, as I was in the middle of a lesson. She ignored me and kept coming. She didn't stop until she was next to my window. I still kept saying no and gesticulated again for her to go away. She asked me to put my window down, I did. At this point, she said she was looking for driving lessons.

I felt really bad and sheepishly handed her a card. She did, however, say she wanted automatic lessons.

My learner was killing herself laughing.

Jackie Bradley, Liverpool

Chapter 1

When to Learn to Drive?

Who was your first driving instructor?

Learning to drive starts a long time before you get behind the wheel for your first lesson. Children observe driving from a very young age and absorb what they see as 'acceptable' behaviour behind the wheel from the adult that drives them around. So, by the time anyone starts their official driving lessons at 17, they have had around 15 years of driver training and education from their loved ones. This could be 15 years of daily driving demonstrations on what rules to break, when to break them, how to break them, how to get away with it, and why they should get away with it! Some parents demonstrate exactly how to get away with bad driving.

This leaves young people fully equipped to become drivers just like them, so when a young person passes their driving test, they may naturally revert to the learnt behaviour they witnessed people getting away with while they were growing up. It could take years of driving lessons to change the behaviours that some learner drivers have witnessed all their lives. To the parents of children who are reading this, please make sure you pass on good driving behaviour to your children when they are your passengers.

Research published by Dr Fiona Fylan showed young people do not recognise that the style of driving used to pass their driving test bears any relation to 'normal' driving. Unfortunately, all the confident experienced drivers they know do not drive like that, so the newly passed young driver reverts to the style of driving which they see as the 'norm' as soon as they pass.

Sadly, when a young person gets it wrong, it sometimes ends in a fatality, either theirs, or an innocent third party.

This is when people like to point the finger at the young driver, but often the young driver who got it wrong has learnt their driving skills from the very people who are there to protect them, their parents. By showing their children bad driving either deliberately or accidentally, repeatedly, their behaviour is then copied. It is this very thing that can instantly take a life.

When is the best time to start your professional driving lessons?

The best time to learn to drive is when you have the money, the time, and the dedication to start and then finish your lessons right through to gaining your driving licence.

Legally, you can drive a car on the public highway in the UK from your 17th birthday. If you get, or have applied for, the enhanced rate of the mobility component of Personal Independence Payment (PIP). You can drive a car when you are 16.

However, you must first have your provisional driving licence that you have signed and features a photograph of you that is less than ten years old. It must also be in date or have a valid date. I mention this because on some provisional driving licences the date hasn't started because you can apply and receive the licence before your 17th birthday, but you can't start your lessons before then, only on, or after your 17th birthday.

You must be able to read a clean number plate in good daylight from 20 metres away for a new style number plate and for the old-style number plate it's 20.5 metres away, this is because on the old-style number plate the letters are slightly bigger. You can of course wear glasses or contact lenses.

If for any reason, you cannot read the number plate on the day of the driving test you will immediately fail the test, and not go out in the car.

It is vital that when you start driving; you take learning to drive seriously and see it as a serious investment. Thinking of the money you are spending as an investment into your future as a skilled driver.

Or, if you are paying for someone else to take their driving lessons, it is the future of their driving you are investing in.

Learning to drive is not cheap nor should it be. Your driving instructor is a professional, with professional driving qualifications.

Why do I mention the cost of a professional driving instructor? Well, I can't tell you the amount of times I've heard people moan about the cost of lessons. But, it is vital before you start lessons you have enough money to continue your training until you pass. Taking a few lessons here and there because they are cheap, or you have been given some money for your birthday is a waste of time if you don't continue, stop/start lessons are never a good thing, even though while you may not have to start from the beginning each time, you will take longer to learn, and in the end, it could cost much more money.

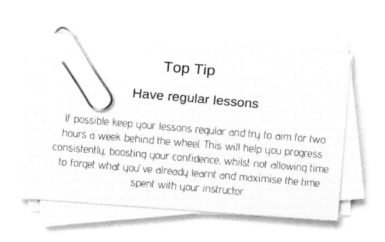

Top Tip

Have regular lessons

If possible keep your lessons regular and try to aim for two hours a week behind the wheel. This will help you progress consistently, boosting your confidence, whilst not allowing time to forget what you've already learnt and maximise the time spent with your instructor.

However, using offers can be a good way of trying out some driving schools or instructors before you part with a large sum of money for a block booking or a course. Watch out for some offers that tie you to an instructor or school. One offer available was 10 lessons for £99. Beware, sometimes the small print says that the lessons must be spread out, meaning you can't take the lessons in succession, with the last two hours of the lessons being used for the driving test day. Some companies have even made pupils keep the last two hours booked for the first two hours of the Pass Plus course - therefore two hours were often never used. So, unless you spend more money with this school you will not get all the hours you paid for. You could end up being stuck with an instructor you simply don't like.

A lady, who I will call Audrey, thought she was getting a good deal with a for £99 offer. Audrey, part way through her hours needed to change her instructor, as the one she had been allocated with was not available on the day of her test. The company in question apparently charged Audrey a £25 'admin fee' to change instructors. Her new instructor told her he had to assess her before allowing her to use his car for the driving test, which is normal practice to be fair, so Audrey had to buy another four hours at the full price costing a further £80. She ended up paying over £100 more than she had expected.

Always, always, read the small print. You are the customer and have every right to change instructors no matter who you are learning with. However, some schools, as we have seen in our story about Audrey, may charge you an admin fee to change driving instructors, which I think is bad practice.

If you were to leave a particular driving school altogether to find another driving school, then you will not be charged an admin fee, you may, of course, lose money if you have bought a special offer that has terms and conditions that either tie you in or prevent you from getting a refund if you are not happy. Driving schools and solo instructors who charge you a professional fee, don't have to have unreasonable terms and conditions in order to make a living.

Investing in Good Training

When someone asks can you do it cheaper!

How much should you expect to pay for driving lessons?

Well, how long is a piece of string? The investment you make in your driving journey is an investment not only for passing the driving test, but for safe and skilled driving for life.

Driving instructors with a professional attitude will use client centred learning to teach their pupils to drive and not just to pass their test, this investment is invaluable. The best driving instructors will help learners recognise their own mistakes and limitations as drivers, and they will also help the learner to self-reflect, self-analyse and self-correct their driving. This is so you can continue to improve your driving well beyond passing your test, not get into lazy habits or allow your driving to fall below the entry level standard that you will have displayed when you passed your test.

Don't always go for the cheapest option when choosing a trainer or instructor.

Imagine using the cheapest, bungee rope that wasn't fastened securely to jump off a 300ft cliff, or the cheapest company who offered you a parachute jump, with very basic training, just enough for you to jump out of the plane, but not including the skills you need if something went wrong. You wouldn't, would you? As with anything and I say it again, you get what you pay for.

For the first few lessons using a special offer is a good idea, but choosing an instructor who is simply giving driving lessons for cost price or below is a bad idea. If you fancy trying an instructor who does not have special offers just book and pay for one lesson. Try not to go for a block booking at first, because this usually means you could be stuck with them, what if you don't like them? You will have to stick with them or possibly lose some of your money.

This brings me to the story of Beryl and Billy, which I hope will explain this; Billy is a very successful driving instructor, he is always full and works a 40-hour week. He always has a waiting list. Billy charges £10 an hour, he grosses £400 per week, which isn't a bad income. Now Beryl, she does not seem to be a very good driving instructor at all, she only really does a 20-hour week, and she does not have a waiting list. Her barrier is her price as it is £20 per hour. But wait, she also grosses £400 per week, the same as Billy, but has a much better work life balance, after all most people who start their own businesses really want more time to spend with their family, and not working six or seven days a week. So yes, book an assessment lesson before you invest in a block booking or course of lessons with an instructor. When adding up the cost of lessons you will have to think about the full cost of a full course, even if you are paying for them one hour at a time. The DVSA suggests pupils will need to take an average of 45 hours with a professional driving instructor, and plenty of private practice, but remember, this is an average, so some people will need more hours and some less. According to First Car magazine, research suggests that it usually takes around 40 hours of lessons with an instructor, plus an extra 20 hours practicing with family or friends. Remember anyone accompanying you has to be 21 or over and have held a full EC/EEA licence for at least the last three years, and of course the correct level of car insurance for you to drive.

10 hours with a substandard driving instructor is simply a waste of money, even at £10 per hour. However, 10 hours with a great instructor is a worthwhile investment, and yes you will pay more than £10 per hour, at current prices it is more like £30 to £35 per hour. Using a great instructor can simply mean you will take fewer hours overall, so the overall cost will end up less. Any quality training will result in a quality outcome.

No matter who you choose to take your lessons with, you will get what you pay for. Learning with an independent instructor is not for everyone, neither is learning with a national or local franchise. I have to say though in our industry 'franchise' seems to be a dirty word and a lot of independent instructors actively encourage franchised instructors to go independent. However, if being on a franchise is so bad, why do so many instructors start on one and choose to stay? I know most of our instructors simply enjoy being part of a team and a brand as together we can do more. It is a bit like encouraging everyone to open up their own independent shop and do away with all the supermarkets, it could just create more competition and not every instructor wants to go solo.

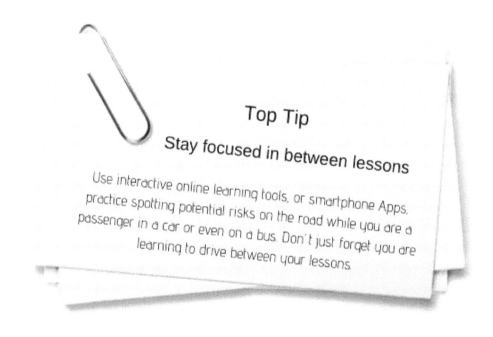

Top Tip

Stay focused in between lessons

Use interactive online learning tools, or smartphone Apps, practice spotting potential risks on the road while you are a passenger in a car or even on a bus. Don't just forget you are learning to drive between your lessons.

Practising the turn in the road.

The pupil moves forward. Keeping the speed nice and slow, really quick steering and excellent observations. Exactly the same as they reversed and the same again as we went forward again.
Pulled them over and complimented them on being able to keep the car nice and slow, really quick steering and excellent observations.
Just one slight problem I said to the pupil.
What is that they asked?
Why are we still facing the same way?
We both had a good laugh, but they didn't make the same mistake again.

Derek Lawton – Newton le Willows

Chapter 2

Choosing an Instructor

Who is the best instructor for you?

How on earth do you choose a great driving instructor? This question is difficult to answer as there are so many variables to think about. In this section I will attempt to dispel a few myths and help you make the right choice for you.

The first thing to look for is whether or not the instructor is legal, and by this, I mean, do they have a driving instructors certificate or licence?

Fully qualified instructors will have a green certificate and trainee instructors have a pink licence, more information in Appendix 2.

Often, very cheap lessons could be offered when an instructor is not licenced. While I can understand why some learners may be attracted to cheap driving lessons, or offers for block booking, or an instructor who their friend took lessons with, to save money, I can't say it enough, money saving should not be your priority when searching for an instructor.

Many people who are looking for driving instructors don't go to the trouble of checking anything at all, and they hardly ever check if the instructor is licensed or not.

In a recent poll (2021) I conducted using social media, 71% of people did NOT know how to tell if an instructor was licenced or not.

So, what do you check for?
Either of these two, below.

A valid dated green certificate or a valid dated pink licence

Either the certificate or licence must be on display in the windscreen while conducting lessons. There are more details in Appendix 2, which you are free to copy or download, use and distribute along with the illegal driving instructor poster in Appendix 3. It is in fact illegal to advertise as a driving instructor or take money for driving lessons unless you are a fully certified driving instructor or licensed as a trainee driving instructor franchised to a driving school.

Trainee driving instructors are not allowed to advertise themselves as instructors or make it look like they are fully qualified, they must be with a driving school and they must get the work through the driving school. Any pupil's recommendations they receive, need to go through the driving school as the driving school must know of all the pupils they are teaching, they must also allow time to continue their training.

I remember hearing about an instructor just after the 2008 credit crunch who was offering lessons in return for electrical goods. If you had a kettle you didn't want, you could exchange it for a 30-minute driving lesson, goodness knows how many lessons a microwave could get you!

Holding a driving instructor's certificate is more than just passing a test. To gain a full certificate, driving instructors have had to pass a three-part rigorous test which takes time, effort, and money to become a fully qualified driving instructor. Before they even get to book their part one of the driving instructors tests, they have to have an enhanced Disclosure and Barring Service (DBS) check which used to be known as Criminal Records Bureau (CRB) check.

There have been people that have been refused entry onto the approved driving instructors register because of what the DBS/CRB checks have revealed. This check came out in 2007 so all the existing driving instructors also had to be checked, there were several removed from the register. Some of the reasons a person may be rejected are serious offences, for example sexual offences, fraud, or serious driving offences.

Illegal instructors may never have been through these checks. They may also have failed their instructor tests, or they have already been rejected. All driving instructors now have to undergo a DBS check every four years, which coincides with their four-year registration as an Approved driving Instructor, which basically is their licence to charge you money.

The part one driving instructor test is in two parts, 100 theory questions and 14 hazard perception video clips. Very similar to the driving theory test but more in-depth. The theory test is where the instructor must prove they have a complete knowledge of road procedure. This test has four areas. The areas are:

- Road procedures
- Traffic signs and signals, car control, pedestrians, mechanical knowledge
- Driving test, disabilities, the law
- Publications and instructional techniques.

Also, on the theory test, is a hazard perception test where the trainee instructor has to do the same as learners and watch 14, one-minute video clips and point out 15 hazards.

ADI Part 1 (Theory Test) Pass mark

Multiple-choice questions:
85 marks out of a possible 100
With a score of at-least 20 out of 25 in the 4 sections.

Hazard perception test:
57 marks out of a possible 75

Once they pass part one of the driving instructors test, they can start part two of the test, where their own driving is tested on all types of roads. They have to continually drive to a very high standard for a minimum of an hour and have to perform all the manoeuvres, including

- Pulling up on the right
- Bay parking, both reversing and driving into a bay.
- Parallel parking
- Emergency stop

Until December 2017 instructors also had to do the reversing to the right, reversing to the left, and turn in the road. They have to read the number plate from a distance of 26.5 meters for vehicles with a new-style number plate and 27.5 meters for vehicles with an old-style number plate. Which is slightly further than the L-test.

The test also includes:

- Independent driving for up to 20 minutes
- Following directions from a SatNav
- Answering five questions from the 'show me tell me' sections found in Appendix 5

They are only allowed six driving faults or minor faults, with no serious or dangerous faults. They can only take this part of the test three times in a two-year period. For every 'show me tell me' question that is incorrect they will score one driving fault, so they must get this right.

Once they have passed the ADI part two, they can then book their ADI Part three, the final part. This is where their instructional capability is tested, this lasts for one hour (45 minutes during the COVID pandemic) and looks at the instructor's ability to help their learner/pupil spot mistakes, analyse mistakes, guide and help the pupil so they can fix the mistakes. (The DVSA records mistakes as faults, however a fault indicates something has been done deliberately where it could just be a genuine mistake.) The instructor will also have to show excellent communication skills, have a good attitude, and be able to alter the level & style of instruction, and change the lesson if required.

Here are the 17 strands that an instructor is tested on. They can only take this test three times in a two-year period.

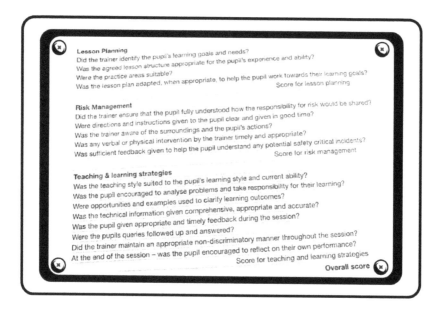

Lesson Planning
Did the trainer identify the pupil's learning goals and needs?
Was the agreed lesson structure appropriate for the pupil's experience and ability?
Were the practice areas suitable?
Was the lesson plan adapted, when appropriate, to help the pupil work towards their learning goals?
                                                            Score for lesson planning

Risk Management
Did the trainer ensure that the pupil fully understood how the responsibility for risk would be shared?
Were directions and instructions given to the pupil clear and given in good time?
Was the trainer aware of the surroundings and the pupil's actions?
Was any verbal or physical intervention by the trainer timely and appropriate?
Was sufficient feedback given to help the pupil understand any potential safety critical incidents?
                                                            Score for risk management

Teaching & learning strategies
Was the teaching style suited to the pupil's learning style and current ability?
Was the pupil encouraged to analyse problems and take responsibility for their learning?
Were opportunities and examples used to clarify learning outcomes?
Was the technical information given comprehensive, appropriate and accurate?
Was the pupil given appropriate and timely feedback during the session?
Were the pupils queries followed up and answered?
Did the trainer maintain an appropriate non-discriminatory manner throughout the session?
At the end of the session – was the pupil encouraged to reflect on their own performance?
                                                   Score for teaching and learning strategies
                                                            Overall score

Reproduced from the ADI Part 3 (SC) with kind permission of the DVSA

Only once they have passed all three parts of the approved driving instructor test, can they call themselves Approved Driving Instructors or an ADI, some instructors refer to themselves as fully qualified driving instructors. Holding an instructor driving certificate, (it is also called an ADI/PDI badge), is so much more than a piece of paper (in fact it's a piece of plastic) and it's absolutely vital that any instructor you are considering holds one.

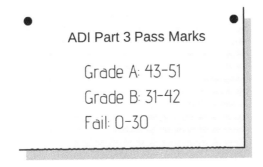

ADI Part 3 Pass Marks

Grade A: 43–51

Grade B: 31–42

Fail: 0–30

I will refer to it as a badge, which I mean either the ADI certificate or the PDI licence.

While conducting driving lessons that are being paid for, the instructor must display their badge in the front windscreen at all times. It must have their photo and an expiry date. It is green with a hexagon shape on one side with the expiry date in the middle, on the other side it has the photo of the instructor which should be no more than four years old. The badge also clearly shows the instructor's name and an expiry date of less than four years. It is signed by the current registrar of the DVSA. (Driving and Vehicle Standards Agency) A picture of both sides of this badge is in Appendix 2.

The badge is issued to the instructor once they send off for it, which can be up to 12 months, after they pass the ADI tests. Afterwards this badge has to be replaced every four years costing the driving instructor, currently £300.

In fact, if they fail to display their badge, they can be fined up to £1000. There is no excuse for an instructor not to display it. Even if they lose it, it can be replaced for just a few pounds from the DVSA.

As I have mentioned there is another type of badge that you might come across which is called the trainee licence or pink badge. It is PINK - no surprises there; it has a triangle on one side. The pink licence is only valid for six months. Check to see if it is out of date, it could be a forgery. The photo should be less than six months old too. Some pink licence holders never get to qualify. If they do not qualify after their third attempt at part three, they have to stop taking money for lessons and give up teaching for money.

If the pink licence expires, again they have to give up teaching. This could also invalidate their driving instructor's car insurance. Some instructors get a second pink licence, this is only given at the discretion of the DVSA ADI Registrar, and it is normally given only if the person has not been able to use the first pink licence, this was prevalent during the COVID-19 Pandemic in 2020, many trainee instructors could not work, and were automatically granted a second pink licence. Instructors who are with a good training establishment who can use the licence fully and are engaged in training should not need a second pink licence. All instructors on a pink or training licence MUST undergo continued training with an ADI Trainer. An image of the pink badge can be found in Appendix 2.

Many insurance companies who specialise in instructor insurance, require evidence that they are insuring a licenced instructor. This proof can be a photocopy of the badge, or the PRN (Personal Reference Number) or the ADI (Approved Driving Instructor) before insurance is granted.

Don't be duped by illegal driving instructors. These instructors probably survive by offering cheap driving lessons, being really friendly but often cutting corners. I would not like to say they are bad people, but they may have never had a DBS check, or it will have run out. They also may not have the correct car insurance. They also use excuses in order not to take you on the day of your driving test because if they took too many people for tests, they would become visible to the authorities. When they take someone for a test, they often pretend they are a family member.

Catching illegal instructors is not easy because the only thing they are doing wrong is charging money for their services. They must be stopped by the police and the DVSA where they will separate the learner and the instructor. Unfortunately, though by this stage the illegal instructor will have formed a pupil-teacher relationship and will have an idea why they are being stopped. They may tell the learner to say they are a friend and they are not paying for the lesson.

Even if the learner tells the authorities how much they are paying for lessons which could mean that the instructor is cautioned by the police, the learner may be reluctant to go to court and testify against him/her. Having said all this, there have been many illegal driving instructors convicted since 2007 when Insight 2 Drive was founded.

Does the gender of your instructor make a difference?

I wasn't sure whether to include this section in the book, as I feel it is the person who counts, not their age, disability, gender, marital status, race, religion or sexual orientation. It is simply the individual and whether or not you 'click' with them.

However, we are often asked whether you should choose a male or female instructor, so I thought it would be worth including here. Some people think female instructors are more caring and more patient than male instructors, but this is not always the case, it is just stereotyping, which we know is wrong. Choosing an instructor based on their sex is a personal choice, it is far better to judge them as an individual and base your decision on who you feel most comfortable with. Consider your own preferred style of learning, are you a visual, audible, or kinaesthetic learner, do you like time to think, reflect, or just get on with it? Choose an instructor who delivers in your preferred style and you simply get on well with.

Top Tip

If your instructor shouts at you –
change instructors!

What's best, a new instructor or an experienced one?

The first thing is to find out what other qualifications or CPD (continued professional development) they have done, as there are new instructors who have already enhanced their skills by continuing to learn and develop as drivers and teachers. Equally, some instructors have been teaching for many years, and yet they never moved on or never updated their skills or looked into current methods of teaching.

Without the instructor updating their skills or doing continued development it would equate to us all still writing on slates, education moves on, and so should driving trainers, or the educators. A police trainer said at a conference that educators should always be educated.

You should look for an instructor with a good attitude to road safety. By this I mean a realistic attitude. There are two ends of the scale here; one is the instructor who does not see that they have anything to do with road safety other than simply teaching the mechanics of driving; and at the other end of the scale, is the instructor who pushes death and destruction down your throat. There must be a balance. However, the possibility of being killed or seriously injured on the road is very real. On average, five people are killed per day on Britain's roads. See driving statistics for seriously injured and killed through road traffic collisions in Appendix 4.

For the new driver, it is not something that is inevitable. Having a realistic attitude to road safety will mean your instructor has given you all the information you need to make the correct choices to keep you and the other road users safe. Once you pass your test, it is down to your skills, your choices, your decisions, and the consequences you may face.

Grading and Pass Rates

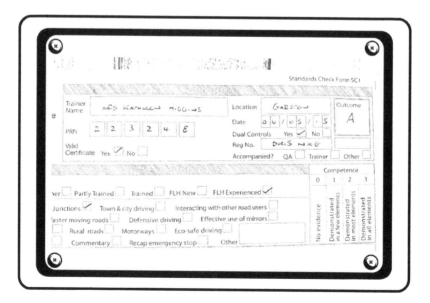

Looking at statistics at face value is a good starter point, however it is flawed. There used to be six grades of instructors.

- Grade 1 – Very Bad - considered dangerous
- Grade 2 – Bad - considered substandard
- Grade 3 – Poor - considered substandard
- Grade 4 – Adequate
- Grade 5 – Good
- Grade 6 – Very Good

Only around 20% of instructors ever got to Grade six. The industry has changed to a two-Grade system, Grade A *(A high overall standard of instruction demonstrated)* or Grade B *(Sufficient competence demonstrated to permit entry to the Register of Approved Driving Instructors)*, as they have tried to bring the grading into line with the rest of education. If a score of 30 or less is obtained, this would be an 'unsatisfactory performance' which would result in a fail.

You might think it's best then to choose a Grade A or a Grade 6 instructor. But it is not as simple as that. I have had nearly 25 years' experience developing driving instructors and have met many instructors who are Grade 4 and Grade B that give fantastic driving lessons, yet fall apart in a test situation. I have also met some Grade 6 and Grade A instructors who tick every box in the standards checklist, but because of being a Grade 6 or A, they have become aloof and self-centred, some of them think that they have no more to learn.

I feel that the standards check itself may be flawed as it is just a snapshot in time, a bit like an MOT, the instructor either gave a fantastic performance on the standards check or not. Whatever the case may be, it is one person's opinion on how that lesson went on that hour, on that day. The instructor's pass rate, pupil testimonials and CPD are simply not considered.

We also have to consider the type of pupils an instructor teaches or specialises in.

For example, there are instructors who have pupils with specific needs or pupils who are not natural learners and may take longer to pass their test.

Let's explore the pass rate. You may see many adverts proclaiming a good pass rate, or 100% pass rate. I once had a 100% first time pass rate. I achieved this by only having three pupils that year and they all passed (first time.) However, one of my team members had taken 30 pupils to test in the same year, with only 24 of them passing the first time. Which makes a first-time pass rate of only 80%, and on paper I am a much better instructor. In reality, I had only three passes where one of my instructors had 24 passes.

Like all statistics, they can be manipulated to show whatever needs to be shown. Having said all that, they must have at least proven they can do the job.

Not all instructors are created equal. There are instructors who are happy to qualify as an instructor and do nothing else. It is a bit like passing your driving test at 17 and getting to 70 and doing nothing to update or improve your driving skill or knowledge. There are instructors out there who continue to develop themselves and keep updated with what is going on in the industry and modern thinking regarding training. There are a few extremes from an instructor who is happy to scrape through their standards check every two years and an instructor who just keeps going on course after course (mentioning no names! But guilty as charged) Some of us simply enjoy learning as much as we enjoy teaching. This all comes at a cost though and there may be instructors who want to go on CPD courses but just cannot afford to. Remember, when you choose an instructor who has furthered their education you will get that extra knowledge and skill which will simply add value to your lessons.

Instructors are trained by instructor trainers; some will have done part one and two on their own before seeking help from a trainer for part three of the test. As mentioned earlier, once an instructor qualifies, they may only have the knowledge, skills, beliefs and values passed on to them from their trainer, especially if they have done no ongoing training themselves.

Once a person has paid for training, especially if they have paid for the full course in one go, they will stick with that training company, even if their gut feeling is telling them something is not right, or the training style does not suit them. I believe training should be done by more than one trainer. At Insight 2 Drive trainees have access to all our trainers, this way they experience different perspectives and added value from each of the trainers. If you are ever not happy with the training you are getting, always speak up, any good training company will listen and take action to address your concerns.

Recommendations are another way to find a driving instructor, always do your research. In the past, people often went with the driving instructor their friends trained with, especially when a friend passed their driving test. There would be little discussion on how many hours it took to get to the test or what the lessons consisted of. Today, you can research on the Internet looking for reviews on social media or Google.

However, please don't just head for the negative reviews. I can only speak for Insight 2 drive; we have suffered some negative reviews from people that have never even trained with us! I am not sure why someone would do this, maybe they are just vindictive or have left the review for the wrong school. On one occasion another driving school owner left us a one-star review, so when I asked them why, it transpired their account had been hacked and left one star reviews for all driving schools in the area! I am glad to say this review was removed. When reading reviews, always read the reply given by the driving instructor or the school and look for differences in how the reviews are written, which should tell you different people have written them.

What's the best car to learn how to drive in?

Top Tip

When buying a new car be aware of the blind spots, different makes have different blind spots

Does the car you learn to drive in make a big difference? No. However, it is important to feel comfortable in the driver's seat, as you could spend the best part of 40 hours in it, not all car seats are suitable for all people.

When we are looking at the size of the car, we are looking at the inside not the outside. The size is more to do with the seating position and what you can see on the road. A bad seating position can lead to fatigue and stresses and strains in the body. A seat that won't adjust to you, for example, not moving forward enough for you to depress the clutch fully to the floor without stretching a bit, can lead to back pain. In fact, if you continue to drive a car with this you can suffer with back pain in later life. Also, it's the same if you are stretching to see out of the windscreen. It will affect your vision, and you will miss what is happening in the far distance. Equally, if your mirrors cannot be set so that you can see comfortably out of the rear, meaning you will quickly stop checking them due to fatigue. This includes the door mirrors too.

They should be adjustable so you can see out of them without straining. I once had a car that wouldn't let me set the nearside door mirror to a position that was best for me. I am only five feet tall, I sit quite far forward in the seat, so the left mirror would not come in far enough for me to get the very best view. I also have difficulty in one particular make of car, where I cannot get the clutch all the way down, so I avoid driving them whenever possible. If a car is too small for you, it could cause physical stress. For example, someone six feet tall learning to drive in a very small car won't work. They will fit in and be able to reach everything, however, they will stoop in the seat to see out of the windscreen and possibly their head will hit the roof on every speed bump. They will also find their knees are too high, which can cause hip problems. If your knees are a lot higher than your hips in the sitting position, not only can you catch your knees on the steering wheel, you are not in a suitable position ergonomically.

You also have to think of the make and model of the car for you, as you must be able to see out of the windscreen clearly and adjust the mirrors so that you can see clearly what is going on around the car. Ensuring you are comfortable in the car seat while you are driving, is another reason it is best to pay for a few lessons first to see before buying a course of lessons.

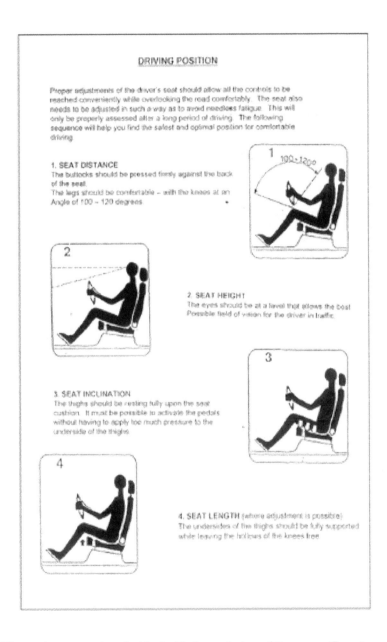

DRIVING POSITION

Proper adjustments of the driver's seat should allow all the controls to be reached conveniently while overlooking the road comfortably. The seat also needs to be adjusted in such a way as to avoid needless fatigue. This will only be properly assessed after a long period of driving. The following sequence will help you find the safest and optimal position for comfortable driving.

1. SEAT DISTANCE
The buttocks should be pressed firmly against the back of the seat.
The legs should be comfortable – with the knees at an Angle of 100 – 120 degrees.

2. SEAT HEIGHT
The eyes should be at a level that allows the best Possible field of vision for the driver in traffic.

3. SEAT INCLINATION
The thighs should be resting fully upon the seat cushion. It must be possible to activate the pedals without having to apply too much pressure to the underside of the thighs.

4. SEAT LENGTH (where adjustment is possible)
The undersides of the thighs should be fully supported while leaving the hollows of the knees free.

Illustrations reproduced with the kind permission of Rosemary Campion.

5. BACK REST ANGLE

The ideal hip angle (with the buttocks fully touching the back rest) is 95 – 115 degrees. It should be possible to handle the steering wheel without constricting the abdomen. The angle between upper arm and trunk should be 20 – 30 degrees and the elbows held at 80 – 120 degrees. The seat back angle should not be greater than 25 – 30 degrees so the head is held erect without straining any muscles.

6. LUMBAR SUPPORT

The sacral vertebrae and upper pelvis must be supported. The lower spine should be as straight and as relaxed as possible with NO hump-back or hollow.

7. CHECK the adjustments made so far.

8. SHOULDER SUPPORT (if included)

A slight contact pressure only is sufficient. On no account must the shoulders be forced into a hunch-back form.

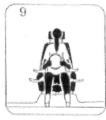

9. SIDE CHECKS (where possible)

An air space of about 1 cm should be left on both sides of the body.

10. HEAD REST

The top of the head rest should be at least level with the driver's eyes, and the space between the head and head rest should not exceed 2 cm.

Illustrations reproduced with the kind permission of Rosemary Campion.

Every Saturday for months, Mary and her mother met me at 2.00 pm at a local hotel. Mary drove a Morris Minor and her mother was always firmly ensconced in the rear seat to keep an eye on proceedings. (Perhaps, she didn't trust me?) After some lessons, I deduced that Mary was totally controlled by her mother. Mary came from a farming background and hygiene was not her top priority. Her white blouse was virtually black as it appeared, she rarely washed herself or her clothes. Apart from that, she was a good pupil. Following every lesson, I would give her a page of the *Rules of the Road* to learn and she had that page off verbatim the following Saturday. Although she couldn't drive herself, Mary's mother was very critical of her driving and continually said she would never pass a driving test as she was stupid. Mary was quite slow to respond to instructions and directions. During lessons, I always gave Mary plenty of time to respond to my directions. One particular Saturday, I asked Mary to take the next road on the right. As she was passing the road, she looked at me and said, "Was that the road you meant?" I replied and said don't worry we'll take the next road on the right. With that, her mother gave her an almighty thump on the back of her head saying "You stupid fool, didn't you hear what the 'boy' said. I quite enjoyed the 'boy' bit, but it was quite an embarrassing moment. However, Mary continued with her lessons and passed her test for the first time. Some weeks later, when I got home for lunch, my wife said a woman in a black shawl called to thank me for helping Mary pass her test. She also gave my wife a pint Lucozade bottle of fresh milk and half a dozen farm fresh eggs as a token of her appreciation.

PS. Mary was the first person I ever saw press the brake pedal with her left foot.

Tom Harrington – Eire

Years ago, I had a lad who could not for the life of him remember to check five tyres without counting his fingers (and thumb). He even counted on his test when asked the tyre tread depth so he could say " I would check all five".

The funny bit - He was doing a PHD in pure mathematics and was a member of Mensa!

Martin Lindsay – Llanelli

Chapter 3

The Chapter for Parents

My Daughter Passing Her Theory Test and Proud Mum Face

Are you thinking of helping your child with their driving?

I simply had to include a chapter for parents in this book. During the 2021 national lockdown I passed a Behaviour Change Course with Dr Fiona Fylan the UK's leading Health Psychologist specialising in road user behaviour, the work I submitted was on trying to change the driving behaviour of the parents in order to keep our children safe on the roads, as it's often the parents who are paying for the driving lessons. I find more often than not parents are disinterested in their child's progress on the lessons, all they do is pay for the lessons and hope for the best. This chapter is especially for you, the parent or guardian, so that you can make sure you end up with a much more well-rounded driver on the road, who will be ready to drive safely for life.

Before reading this chapter, please reread the chapter, 'When do we learn to drive?' It's a sad fact that young people don't always see a connection between how they drive on a driving test and how they drive afterwards. As mentioned in that chapter 'all the experienced and confident drivers they know simply do not drive like that'. I have repeated this here as it is so important. Before you formally teach your child how to drive or give them some private practice between their professional lessons that they are taking with a driving instructor, it is important that you recognise that some things may have changed since you learnt to drive. Having taken my driving test back in the 1980s I can testify to this.

I have been involved in the driver training and education industry since the 1990s. I can say there have been massive improvements on driving styles, rules, regulations and vehicle design, so as you probably know, driving the modern car is very different to the one you may have learnt to drive in. Of course, there are also driving instructors who may well be old-fashioned in their teaching styles and have not moved with the times themselves. I can remember countless times I have taken a pupil on that had been learning with someone else, and they would change down the gears sequentially, instead of using block gear changes or selective changes. I would ask if their last instructor was an older person, the answer was more often than not 'yes'. Just to point out though, not all older driving instructors are stuck in their ways. I am one of the 'older ones' now!

All good driving instructors will be happy for you to sit in on some of your child's lessons in order for you to see what goes on in the modern driving lesson. In fact, some will even offer you a one-to-one training session and pass on some tips on how to help the learner progress their driving in the best way if you are helping them with private practice between lessons.

Once the learner has mastered car control and is confident to drive a car without dual controls, with the agreement of the learner, their instructor and you, it is better for them to get some extra practice. This is not to try to save money on training, it is more to do with getting that extra mileage while being supervised and instilling good habitual behaviour. During driving lessons, it is impossible to come across every scenario that the new driver is going to face on the road, so getting private practice will help them simply come across more situations, the more miles they do the more situations they will face, while they have help. It is vital that whoever is supervising them does not disagree with the professional driving instructor or try to teach different styles, the instructor will know what level of driving and style is required to pass today's UK driving test. If you have any concerns or disagree with anything, speak to the driving instructor, they will explain the 'why' factor and put your mind at rest.

Please also avoid the words, 'in my day' and 'when I learnt to drive, we...' If you are in doubt about anything simply ask the driving instructor. The good ones will not take offence or get upset because you asked. They will know as I do, that there have been some changes and no doubt more changes to come. If you are still unsure about something and you have chosen a driving school as opposed to a driving instructor who just works for themselves, then you can ask the school owner, who is likely to be a driving instructor or has been a driving instructor. You can consult The Official DVSA Guide to Driving - the essential skills.

The important thing to remember is that all learners will make mistakes. We all make mistakes no matter how experienced we are as drivers, so what chance do the people who are just learning the skill have? And guess what? This is absolutely fine; mistakes are often the best way to learn.

Top Tip

A mistake is education in disguise

I do not mean mistakes that are likely to endanger anyone. Remember when you are supervising, you share responsibility for the risk. In fact, you are legally responsible and deemed in charge of the vehicle. But the small mistakes such as stalling at traffic lights, going slowly, turning into a side road and being hesitant moving out of a side road are all common mistakes which, although need to be addressed, can be a minor inconvenience to other road users.

Being over-controlling or over-helpful can be counterproductive and cause the learner to take a backwards step while learning to drive. I have witnessed this happening in an advanced driving session I once had the pleasure of observing. To be fair the person giving the instruction wasn't a fully qualified driving instructor but a willing volunteer, and possibly had very little training for this role, but he was doing his best, and genuinely trying to help. The driver in question was a lady, who I'll call Irene. She was training with me to become a driving instructor and she was also doing her advanced test at the same time. Irene told me that in her advanced lesson she was being given conflicting information on what is considered best practice. At this point I must stress that there are minor differences between advanced driving and ADI Part 2, (which is what Irene was working towards with me.) They are tested slightly differently, but on the whole both require a smooth, controlled, progressive drive with a quiet efficiency, within the law. Or to put it another way, being in the right position, at the right speed, in the right gear for the conditions. So, back to this conflicting information. Irene wasn't a terrible driver at all, and we had already put her in for her test, but on the day of her advanced driving session, she simply lost it. The observer was over critical and massively over-instructing. She was being told when to look, what lane to be in, what mirrors to check and even what gear to be in, ALL THE TIME!

Top Tip

Brakes to Slow, Gears to Go!

We don't teach changing down through the gears anymore, we just use the brakes to slow the car down first then choose the appropriate gear to drive on again.

This stopped Irene's natural thought process in its tracks, she became a blithering wreck, who couldn't wait for the session to end.
I remained professional throughout the hour, even thanking the observer for an interesting session.

Going back to helping our children. They are still learning and prone to making mistakes they rarely make. Let's give them a break folks, work with them and equally important, work with their professional instructor. Help them, but don't crush their confidence or over instruct or you might end up with an 'Irene' in the driving seat.
It is vital that you remember to make sure you have the correct insurance in place when a learner driver is having driving lessons in

your car. You may also find that your car insurance premium, if they are going to drive your car, could go up after they have passed their test, because they will now drive unsupervised and possibly with friends. There are insurance companies who use telematics or black box technology. These are systems that allow the driver to drive at any time, some restrict when you can drive, for example late at night or early morning. Most measure speed, cornering and braking. The best ones I feel are the ones that look at the overall style of driving and not penalise the driver for one-off actions.

For example, the telematics shows when the driver is braking really hard or accelerating too fast so the driver could pay for this by being charged a higher insurance premium. There are occasions even the best drivers have to take some sort of evasive action in order to avoid a collision. If this happens once, the insurance company will not record this but if it's happening on a daily basis, then something is wrong with the driving style. Some systems charge more if a driver has to drive at night too, some even prohibit night-time driving, so make sure you sign up to the correct one.

A key point to remember is that if someone else drives this car, such as a parent or partner, and drives badly they will affect the insurance premium, because the insurance company doesn't know who is driving.

Another consideration is how much money is received up front. Some insurance companies want you to pay a high premium up front and then they will give you a discount for driving well. Others assume you are going to drive well so will give you the discount first and then charge you more if you don't drive well.

Never say you are the main driver of your child's car, this is called fronting and is considered fraud, so it's against the law. The consequences are severe, you may...

- Have your policy cancelled or voided.
- Get up to six points put on your licence
- Be issued with a hefty fine
- End up with a driving ban.

All of which will put your insurance up, possibly far more than the money you are trying to save. The main driver should be the person who drives the car most of the time.

I am in favour of telematics systems, and I believe we should all have one because it will then be the careless drivers who will pay more for their insurance and rightly too. However, as a result, the drivers who can afford the higher premiums, may feel they have paid for the right to drive badly. As you can see, it's important to do some research as choosing the wrong one can restrict the driver's choice of employment. Which leads me to ask, does this lead to automation?

I was twenty and in my second car. My dad was upgrading his and gave me his old car, a Renault Fuego 1.6 GTX. It was quite a quick car for its size and not bad looking either and I loved it, so did my mates. However, the car lasted about six weeks in my hands before I smashed it into a tree.

There are a few reasons why I crashed.
1. I was driving too fast
2. I was having a laugh with my driving
3. I didn't anticipate the road conditions
4. I was not prepared to drive that car

It was Sunday lunchtime; I had been playing football and was driving my friend home. He already warned me to slow down, but the sun was out, the music was on and I was really enjoying myself. About 2 miles after dropping him off, I overtook a car on a country road I know really well, Brookhill Lane coming out of Pinxton, and on the bend facing Brookhill Hall my car met its demise as I smashed it into a tree, I think I was doing about 60mph. The car I overtook, well, that passed me by and didn't stop and I must have banged my head because a horse who was being expertly ridden on the other side of the road, started to ask me if I was ok. Yes, the horse asked me. I was very lucky that day, I didn't have a scratch on me, but the car was written off and it was at least another year before I could get another one and it was nowhere near as nice as my dad's old car.

David Pool – France

Chapter 4

Which Instructor or School Should You Choose?

Where on earth do you start?

There are many types of driving schools to choose from; national driving schools that cover most of the country, local driving schools are generally smaller, but they cover a local or specific area. Finally, local independent instructors who work on their own. The question is, should you choose a large national driving school, a local multi-car school or an independent driving instructor?

Let's dispel a few myths. Most driving instructors are self-employed and either work on their own, join a small to medium local school under a franchise agreement or work under a franchise for a national driving school.

Pros and cons:

Once you have an instructor, you will base your opinion on the driving school on how well you like the instructor you ended up with. And more importantly how safe and comfortable you feel with them, and if their car suits you. But what are the advantages and disadvantages of having one or the other?

The national school:

Instructors who work with a large national school will have the backing of a large well-known brand with a skilled and dedicated in-house marketing team, and usually a bigger advertising budget than most local schools or independent instructors. One national school I know of, doesn't spend on traditional advertising anymore but simply invests in great SEO (search engine optimisation) so that they rank first place organically in searches for driving lessons. They have connections with TV and radio as they usually feature in most of the national news articles. Individual instructors working with the national school, will of course get their own recommendations and are encouraged to do so.

Some instructors, and I stress some, may not have the same level of customer service as an independent driving instructor, because if they lose a pupil, the national school will swiftly and easily find a replacement pupil. Not all national schools are the same, one national school will pass a pupil to an instructor then the instructor will go to the back of the 'pupil allocation' queue, so they then have to wait their turn before getting another pupil, so this could encourage the instructor to look after their pupils.

Another consideration is the franchise fee the driving instructor has to pay to the driving school. This fee may be expensive, but there is a lot more to it than that, national schools need to survive so they have to make their fees, whether it is a pupil allocation fee, a full franchise with a car or what is known as a 'headboard' franchise, which does not include the car. Any fees incurred in any business is usually passed on to the end customer, you, the learner. Instructors who work with a national school will also be in a tight contract, so they have to make sure they work enough hours to pay their weekly or monthly fees, they cannot just park the car up and have a long lunch.

These instructors will have full back office support to help them run their business and take their inbound calls. This means they can just focus on giving great lessons without interruptions, so, although they will still have to update their diary and do their accounts, they don't have to worry about where their next pupil will come from or where to advertise. In addition, the car may be supplied as part of the franchise and will be maintained by the driving school and replaced at regular intervals, which means you are learning in a newer car with all the modern technology, etc.

How about taking lessons with an independent driving instructor?

Learning with an independent driving instructor may ensure you get a more personalised service.

Many of them will take extra care and look after their customers as they have no guarantee of a steady stream of pupils, so word of mouth from happy pupils will be a part of their business plan. Independent instructors will make all the decisions for their driving school, such as what prices to charge, what advertising to do. Although, some of their time may be spent multitasking, for example taking bookings between driving lessons or grabbing lunch between lessons. Some instructors even keep their mobile phone on and speak to other pupils or take bookings during a driving lesson. They will also have to do all the marketing, telephone calls, booking, and chasing pupils themselves, at which time they cannot earn money, they may also not have a healthy work life balance.

They do have the flexibility to choose to take a day off or a long lunch without having to worry about meeting a franchise payment. It has to be said that there are products and services to help and support the independent driving instructor and can help them with some of this back-office work, for example, taking phone messages. However, all these services still have to be paid for. Some independent instructors forget about the hidden costs of depreciation, road fund licence, insurance, servicing, not having a temporary vehicle available, etc. Some purchase older second-hand cars, which makes it more cost effective for the instructor, but some pupils just don't want to take lessons in an older vehicle. Reliability can become an issue with older vehicles too. This could be why many instructors choose to stay in partnership with a driving school. The extra work and time in running their driving school could be spent giving lessons and earning money and achieving a better work life balance.

If you have a problem with an independent instructor, there is no backup, maybe you have prepaid for lessons and the instructor does not deliver the lessons, or just simply runs off with your money, you may have nobody to complain to. There is an option to report them to the DVSA (Driving and Vehicle Standards Agency), but then it can become your word against theirs. Normally, the only type of complaints the DVSA will get involved in, is cases of misconduct of the driving instructor, such as inappropriate behaviour towards their pupils. Please don't let any of the above put you off an independent instructor, I know some fantastic ones.

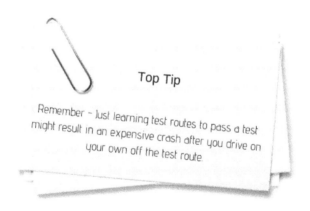

Top Tip

Remember – Just learning test routes to pass a test might result in an expensive crash after you drive on your own off the test route.

Local multi-car driving schools

As you can imagine I am biased here because I am the owner of a local multi-car driving school, Insight 2 Drive. So, for balance I'll start with the negative points in the local multi-car school: We cannot compete with the marketing and instructor availability of a national school. We don't have the money to spend on technology, apps etc. that large schools do. Which means potential pupils, especially those who are new to an area and may not be aware of the local driving school but will recognise the branding of a national school. You could say that a national driving school is like a chain of hotels or coffee shops. You know what to expect when you use one of these chains, unlike the local coffee shop or hotel, but may adjust to your needs faster. However, while the products and services in a large chain of coffee shops may all be the same, it is the staff that can make all the difference to your experience. It is similar with multi-car driving schools, either local or national, the individual instructors will make the biggest impact on your experience.

So, even a local school is at the mercy of the driving instructors. Most local schools' will vet the instructors who work with their team, but with the best will in the world, people are people, and the franchisor cannot keep tabs on the instructors all the time.

In my driving school I have trained or partly trained all of the driving instructors who work in our team, but I cannot say the same for other schools.

The best thing about learning with a local small school is that the school owner will be very customer focused as they don't have the marketing budget or a skilled team of marketers that the big national driving schools have, so every customer is treated like gold. Plus, most local schools will not keep working with an instructor who loses pupils at a high rate or is negatively affecting the reputation of the driving school. Remember, everyone gets things wrong from time to time, my view is that it is more important to focus on what is done to rectify the mistake, that matters the most.

Another benefit of a multi-car school is, if something goes wrong with the instructor, you have someone to talk to or complain to, other than the instructor themselves. You can also pay the school directly for your driving lessons or courses, safe in the knowledge that your money is safe as it should not be paid to the instructor until you have had your lesson.

You can swap instructors within the local school. You can also ask for another instructor from the driving school to conduct a mock test, this can usually be done without incurring an admin charge. Insight 2 Drive does not charge for this. Be aware that some national schools may charge an administration fee for changing instructors or using a different instructor to conduct a mock test, but this does not apply to all of them.

At Insight 2 Drive, we work very much as a team. For a team to be successful, I believe all team members have to share the same beliefs and values, work well together and share their skills and knowledge. If an instructor joins us and does not fit in with the values of the company and the rest of the team, we quickly part company, as we only want instructors who want to be with us. It is simply not healthy for the instructor, the team or the company if they stay with us.

We hold monthly meetings and have many social events which help us work together in the common aim of making your journey to a successful driving test pass, a pleasant and memorable experience. We try to keep our franchise fees as low as possible to try to make sure the instructors that want to stay with us can afford to, it also goes some way to encourage the instructors to work together as a team. No matter who you choose to train with, they must suit you as an individual. Always check the reviews, however, large national schools will get more reviews than your independent instructor, because as a whole they will teach more learners at any one time. The key point to remember is that anyone can get a critical review or get a bad one posted by an unknown person, who may have never even used your services.

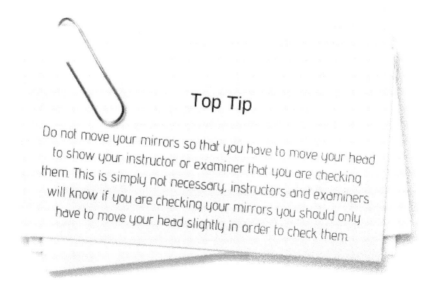

Top Tip

Do not move your mirrors so that you have to move your head to show your instructor or examiner that you are checking them. This is simply not necessary, instructors and examiners will know if you are checking your mirrors you should only have to move your head slightly in order to check them.

Should you choose an instructor with extra qualifications?

As I have mentioned in the previous chapter. The simple answer is yes, as this shows the instructor has pride in their own development and can often pass that extra learning back to you. Although, make sure the instructor's attitude matches their qualifications. I have known instructors who have lots of advanced driving qualifications, and once they passed, they simply reverted to their old driving style.

In fact, I have the experience of one driving instructor who gave me a lift to a meeting. He was driving his school car, carrying his school logos. I commented on his speed and the fact that he was driving constantly above the speed limit. I knew this instructor had just passed all but one of the advanced driving tests.

He asked me, "Don't you have two styles of driving? One for tests and one for when you are driving off duty?"

I couldn't help but think about the attitude he must have been passing onto his pupils. I never got in his car again.

Depending on what CPD your instructor has undergone will depend on what extra info you get. I can remember many years ago I used to teach driving into a parking bay, rural roads, and while teaching driving instructors, how to teach these things, even though they were not tested on the L-test or on the part three test back then. As an advanced driver myself I have more than one perspective on 'best practice' in driving. For example, asking a young person not to drive too fast on rural roads is pointless, they are more than likely going to do it, so why not teach them how to keep the vehicle balanced and at the right speed, in the right gear and the right position on the road for maximum safety and control.

Simple information on why we have 20mph speed limits and zones can also instil a greater understanding of why we have these low speed limits. Instructors who are taught the bare minimum can only pass the bare minimum on to you. Frequently, when working with trainee instructors, I hear them say "This is a 30 zone as it is a built-up area". They simply do not explain how to tell it is a built-up area or why it has a 30mph limit. A built-up area is any road with street lights, which denote a 30mph speed limit, it does not have to have buildings.

Every extra bit of knowledge and skill will only help you stay safe and skilled on the road, as well as staying out of trouble with the police.

There are some instructors who are involved with local road safety projects, our local one is called Engage which was developed by Cheshire and Merseyside Road Safety Partnership.

This is where you will get loads of quality tuition, especially focused on future proofing your driving, exploring your attitude and behaviour. The Engage modules are...

- Driving to the conditions
- Driving under the influence
- Refuelling & car maintenance
- Other road users
- State of mind & distractions
- Speed awareness
- Driving when tired
- Driving with passengers
- Impulse control

Insight 2 Drive has been involved with Engage for many years and watched it develop and grow in strength. I have put a link to the website in Appendix 9.

Another one to look out for is 'The Honest Truth' which was developed in the South West of England. It comes from a different perspective than Engage. Again, you will get extra training on these factors. The Honest Truth is now run by FirstCar. There is a link in Appendix 9.

- Distractions
- Drink driving
- Drugs
- Insurance
- Mobile phones
- Seatbelts
- Showing off
- Speeding
- Tiredness
- Vulnerable road users

Any road safety initiative your instructor is involved with must be positive as it shows their willingness to go the extra mile in order to keep their learners safe and skilled on the road for life.

So how do you tell? One clue could be that your instructor just keeps going on about the driving test, saying things like; you need to do this for the test, or do that for the test. If you are asking questions that are not being answered, then it might be the case that your instructor has not had adequate training or has not developed themselves since qualifying.

Another indication is that you are kept on test routes all the time and being shown how to negotiate the junctions within the test routes and not being helped to think for yourself. Once you pass, you are unlikely to stick to test routes.

If you have any doubts speak to your instructor or the driving school if you are with a multi-car school.

Top Tip

With anything in life – the more we hurry the more mistakes we make – driving is no exception!

Instructor mistakes or misconceptions to watch out for

How much longer do I need to listen to this briefing?

Here are some things instructors may say or do to make as much money as possible from you, without giving you effective and proactive training, or to be fair, just might not know any better.

I would like to see them as mistakes instructors make rather than think an instructor would do this on purpose to 'trick' someone. Just remember when reading this section, I am talking about a minority of instructors, there are some fantastic instructors out there working independently or with national and local schools. There may well be some instructors out there who unwittingly do one of these things as this is how they have been taught to do it, or have simply taken incorrect advice from another instructor, they have just been guided in the wrong direction.

➔ One of the common mistakes is to take you to a road or into an environment you are not ready for. For example, taking you onto a busy or fast road as part of your early driving lessons. If you have the skill base in place and are emotionally ready this will not be a problem. However, if you are not ready, which is more often than not, your experience will be a negative one. This can cause a massive knock to your confidence as a driver. As a result, you might need to take extra lessons in order to regain the confidence and get rid of the negative emotions instilled in the early lesson. For some drivers this feeling never goes away, and although they may hold it together for the duration of their driving test, and actually pass, they may never be a confident driver and may never learn to enjoy driving.

➔ Another, sadly common, mistake is to put the learner driver into your test too early. The instructor may know their learner has little or no chance of passing, or the learner or learners' parents may have pressured them to put them in for the test. They will push ahead, even knowing that there is a risk of their car being damaged. I know of one driving school car that ended up on its roof after only five minutes into the driving test. This could of course have been the fault of the other driver. For the learner driver this will be the first time they have driven without help. This is a horrible experience, and they will come back into the test centre with a failure or have the embarrassment of having the test abandoned for reasons of public safety. If the test is abandoned, some examiners will leave the pupil in the car while they walk back to the test centre or get a lift back from another examiner who is not out on a test. If the distance is not too far the pupil and the examiner may walk back to the test centre together, then the pupil will have to walk back to the car with the instructor. Not a pleasant experience whatever way it happens!

Even worse, they could actually pass! Now, this will be a shock to the driving instructor and a delight to the newly qualified driver. Regrettably, they will not realise they have been short-changed until they are driving solo, and they feel that they have only been taught the bare minimum skills required. The question then is, will you or any other learner that has passed the driving test this way, be a confident and skilled driver who is in fact contributing to safer roads?

Putting the learner in for their test too early will damage their confidence and they may have to take even more driving lessons to build that confidence back up. Another reason for a pupil taking their driving test before they are ready is that the instructor may simply not know if the pupil is ready or not, so they are using the driving test as a very expensive 'mock' test. Most reputable driving schools will conduct a mock test for you, if they feel it necessary, and also with a different driving instructor, to better get the feel of the driving test.

→ By far the most common mistake is to keep the car parked up at the side of the road while giving the learner unnecessary, lengthy and over complex explanations on how the car works. I have seen some driving school cars parked up for over 40 minutes without moving at all. There should be no reason to be stopped for this length of time. I must stress that stopping during the lesson is vital in order to explore feedback, review the lesson and check the learners' goals are being met, this is in fact, marked on the driving instructors test of their instructional ability and subsequently every two to four years on their standards check. If they don't give good feedback during their session, they can fail their test too. The stops during a lesson should be only a few minutes at a time. I believe we should aim to use five minutes at the start of a lesson, five minutes at the end and some stops for feedback and or praise during the lesson. This not only gives the pupil a short break, it allows time to review the goals set. During an hour lesson there should be at least 40 minutes of actual driving. There will be pupils with a learning style that this will not suit, and they may need more time at the side of the road. Therefore, the instructor should always adapt to the learner's skill level and learning style.

→ Getting the learner moving off and stopping too early can also be a disaster. I have personal experience of this happening. One instructor who I knew said 'they always used the pedals without the learner knowing. They leave the lesson thinking I am fantastic because I got them driving on their first lesson'. This is wrong, the instructor is cheating the learner into thinking you have done a good job. Some of these learners will have difficulty dealing with the transition that has to be made for them to be able to use the foot controls for themselves, which may take them longer to learn. If the learner knows their instructor is using the dual controls because they want to 'chunk down' or break the task up into little steps, where the instructor will be responsible for the speed of the car and the learner is responsible for the steering and mirrors etc., if this is agreed and is helping the learner reach their goals for that lesson, then great. If the learner does not know the instructor is using the dual controls and is being 'cheated' then it is not a good thing at all. Of course, if they ever change instructors, they soon realise that they cannot do as much as they thought they could. I have taken on many learners who have told me they could do everything and had 30 driving lessons, but they couldn't even move the car away from the roadside without help.

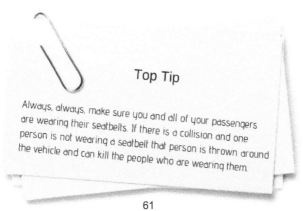

Top Tip

Always, always, make sure you and all of your passengers are wearing their seatbelts. If there is a collision and one person is not wearing a seatbelt that person is thrown around the vehicle and can kill the people who are wearing them.

→ One common myth is that some instructors will tell the learner how many lessons they will need before they have even seen them drive. There is no way of knowing for sure as this is a very individual thing. Some learners will learn the controls of the car really quickly but find traffic management or reading the road a challenge. Others will struggle with reversing or parking. Some will struggle with controls but read the road very well. Everybody is different. Most new learners or beginners will usually need over 10 hours. Others may need fewer hours because they have been driving with mum or dad, so they just need a brush up on the lessons with a driving instructor. Some parents have a very selective memory of their own lessons, with many telling their children that they only had 10 lessons and passed the first time. They forget how many hours they practiced with their parents.

As a learner, I remember driving all the way from the M6, junction 36 Kendal to Millom with my dad, he had one hand on the steering wheel and the other one on the handbrake; I am sure it was not a pleasant experience for him. It must be said that the driving test today is very different, and in order to pass the modern test, the first time, you will have to drive consistently well for the full 40-minute test, including following a SatNav or road signs.

Driving schools can, of course, have their own rules on minimum lessons they would like you to have with them. There are few instructors that will take a learner just for their driving test. This is because the learner will drive the instructor's car, so the instructor has to know that the learner can drive consistently well, keeping their car and everyone safe, before agreeing to let the learner use the car for their test.

There is no hard rule that you have to have over 10 hours of lessons before taking your test. There are people who by the time they take lessons with an instructor have already been driving since a young age, some legally on private land, some will have been riding mopeds or motorcycles, some doing many hours with parents and some even illegally on public roads. The best way to find out is to book an assessment lesson with an instructor and go from there, even then it is your choice how many hours you do, or how many hours you pay for up front with that individual instructor, after all you are the customer.

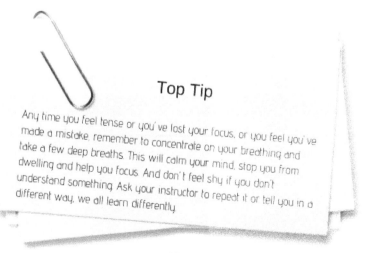

Top Tip

Any time you feel tense or you've lost your focus, or you feel you've made a mistake, remember to concentrate on your breathing and take a few deep breaths. This will calm your mind, stop you from dwelling and help you focus. And don't feel shy if you don't understand something. Ask your instructor to repeat it or tell you in a different way, we all learn differently.

I was told by my father when I was a teen and learning to drive – to
"Get that signal off quick! The bulb will go!"
Another -
"Hold the indicator stick or you'll snap it off if you keep flicking it with your finger"
Another -
"Get that radio off and all your heaters, they are only there to run your battery down". I used to wear two jumpers under my coat after that. Terrified for my brand-new battery to lose its edge, as I used my demister or warmed the car. I brought out a portable battery radio whenever I went for a drive … just in case my dad was right!

Anonymous

An elderly farmer contacted me for some lessons as his driving test was coming up. He was a very nice man who insisted I sit on the rear of the tractor. Although it was quite a big tractor it wasn't the most comfortable place to sit. (In retrospect I shouldn't have done so). On the first lesson, he arrived with his nephew in tow. His licence had expired and he wasn't entitled to a second one. No problem, he said, I have two farms and I can give the address of the second farm, so the licensing authority won't know it's me. As he had no provisional licence, we concentrated on the Rules of the Road and hand/arm signals. On the day of the test, he arrived in good time. The examiner explained the procedure. He would follow the tractor and when he sounded the horn he was to pull in and await further instructions. Instead of stopping the farmer opened the throttle and sped off. The examiner waited for some time and then returned to the office. After about forty-five minutes, the farmer arrived back at the test centre saying:

"Everything went fine; I drove up through the belly of the town and had no problems whatsoever. Give me the piece of paper so I can get my full licence". Needless to say, the examiner was unable to give him the Certificate of Competence.

Tom Harrington – Eire

Chapter 5

Your Driving Lessons

As discussed under 'Learner beware - common instructor mistakes' point 5, Instructors can give you an approximate idea of how many lessons you will need, as there is no minimum or maximum. Always watch out for the word 'lesson' as this could mean anything, from 10 minutes to four hours. This is the same when asking for prices, as most instructors tell you their per hour rate. Always ask how long the lesson is. I know of one local school whose lessons are 45 minutes with a double lesson being 90 minutes, so you could get two hours for the same price. The DVSA reported it took on average, 45 hours of professional instruction and plenty of private practice to pass the UK driving test on the first attempt, again remember this is the average.

Driving lessons are not cheap and nor should they be. There are lots of overhead costs that an instructor has to factor in when deciding what to charge per lesson. The costs that need to be considered are the car itself, either purchased or leased, the road fund licence and fuel. The average mileage for a driving lesson is around 15 to 20 miles. Plus, MOT tests, breakdown cover, car cleaning, insurance, which is approximately £600 and can be in excess of £1000 and possibly gap insurance on top of this. They also need to factor in the franchise's cost, public liability and professional indemnity insurance, professional memberships, administration costs, telephone costs, the ADI/PDI badge, which cost £300 for the ADI badge every four years and £140 for the PDI badge which lasts only six months. Good instructors will also pay for their own CPD and training. Then there is marketing and advertising, some of these costs will be part of the franchise fees, but not all, independent instructors although they won't have the franchise fee to pay, they will have to pay for everything else. All this has to be considered when they set their prices. The instructor also has to plan for holidays, pension, sickness and being forced off the road by bad weather, remember, they don't get paid when they are not giving lessons.

Apparently, people will pay more for a piano lesson than a driving lesson, plus you would have to supply the piano. Tennis lessons are more expensive than driving lessons. I have yet to hear about anyone who has been killed by a rogue piano or an out-of-control tennis ball!

Ask yourself, if you were in a taxi and driving around for an hour, how much would it cost?

What to Expect During Your First Driving Lessons?

Your first lesson should comprise some sort of introduction and explanation of the course you are embarking on. It is important to recognise that you are starting a course of driving lessons, having a single lesson is of no use to anyone. How you organise your driving course is up to you, one hour per week, a few lessons a week, or an intensive course which is several many hours of driving each day, for several consecutive days, it's up to you what suits you best. I do have advice on this, but I'll come back to the best ways to structure your driving course in a later chapter.

On your first lesson the instructor may drive you to a training area. On the journey the instructor will use this time to discuss your goals for the lesson, the outcomes you would like and what type of help you feel you would like from your instructor; they may also want to find out a bit about you, your hobbies, work and interests, this often can help the instructor with your preferred learning style and help the instructor relate some things on the lessons to information you already know. Most of your first lesson should be you behind the wheel.

As an instructor myself, I make sure that you have a good understanding of all the main controls of the car, either helping you from scratch or checking the knowledge and understanding you already may have, so we can keep everybody safe. I remember, when participating in a charity event as an ADI, I drove a police car around a track, but before moving off the police trainer asked me to show him which pedal was the brake. I was slightly offended, but he said he had never seen me drive before, so for his own safety he needed to check. However, you don't need demonstrations for the radio, cruise control or heating, as these can be explained when you need them. If it is raining on the first lesson it might be necessary to demonstrate how to operate the windscreen wipers.

A quote from a very experienced examiner, who examines driving instructors on their test of instructional ability, said,

"If the footwork is not right, then the rest of the lesson cannot be right." This means that it is vital that you can control the car, once you can control the car your instructor will talk you through or out of most situations.

There are some instructors who use the turn in the road or three-point turn to teach steering and clutch control. I feel this is putting too much pressure on the learner driver. It takes just 10 minutes for most people to master clutch control in a focused lesson, not an hour. An hour driving lesson is usually broken down into 10 to 15-minute lessons.

Practice, practice, practice.

Once you've gained some experience with an instructor, if possible, get a friend or relative to take you out for extra practice on the road. One of the key ingredients of driving is gaining experience which brings with it confidence. So spend as much time as you can behind the wheel. Remember, there are rules about who can accompany a learner, they must be over 21 and have had a full licence for over 3 years. Importantly please make sure you have the relevant insurance in place, too.

Theoretically, once you have learnt the controls you can learn the rest of the basic skills in any order. The order those basic skills are taught in should ideally be up to you, with the advice and help of your instructor.

Many years ago, I was coaching a young chap on his very first lesson. I asked him if he knew anything about the controls of the car; he said no, I asked what was the first thing he would like to know about. He replied he would like to know how to use the windscreen wipers. It was a dry, summer day. I said we couldn't use the windscreen wipers because the windscreen is dry, and the wipers could drag dust across the windscreen and scratch it, but I could show him how to clean the windscreen.

We did that, and from that minute onwards he was quite happy with the rest of the lesson, because using the windscreen wipers must have been playing on his mind, so, once we got that out of the way he was able to concentrate on the rest of his lesson.

Some basic skills need sub-skills to be mastered first, for example, if a learner wanted to learn the emergency stop, which is now called the controlled stop. In one of the first lessons it is vital to learn the sub-skills of the emergency stop first. Some instructors will leave the emergency stop until the day before the driving test, this I feel, is far too late and in my experience teaching it early gives the learner a sense of control and confidence that they know how the car reacts. Plus, they also know they can stop the car quickly if they need to. Instructors who leave teaching this until closer to the driving test have told me they have had their pupils perform the emergency stop inappropriately. This raises the question of why the pupil feels the need to stop quickly and why the instructor isn't helping the learner driver become proactive and not reactive. Any instructor can be caught out, but part of the standards check is to make sure the instructor is aware of their surroundings and the pupils' actions. Human behaviour dictates that when one feels threatened or is not in control, we stop thinking logically and react impulsively. This is the flight or fight response, when we feel threatened or feel we are in danger we will do one of three things, either run away, fight or the third one is to freeze in the hope the predator does not see us. None of these responses are good for driving. I have experienced a pupil freeze at the wheel; they kept driving straight even though we were heading for someone's front garden! Luckily, I stopped the car safely, so we averted any off-roading.

Here is a list of some basic controls taken from our pupil learning pack.

Once you have mastered the basic skills and you can perform them to a good level consistently, it makes the next section easy for you to learn, as junctions and almost everything else is a combination of the basic skills done at the correct time and in the correct order.

For example, if you can move a car off a hill then all you need to do is perform the same at a junction. Why wait to learn hill starts, when you are at the end of the road with a stream of cars behind you? After you master your car control and gain confidence in this, the next logical steps in learning to drive would be junctions. Depending where you are starting your lessons from, will depend on what junctions you are going to learn and master first.

Here are the junctions; the boxes are ticked when 'introduced' 'prompted' and 'independent'.

It makes sense in an ideal world to get used to turning left first, both turning into roads and emerging out. Most instructors will, when teaching junctions for the first time, drive you to a suitable location, this will make the most of your lesson rather than struggling to move away from your own location, which could be a busy street or area of town.

Historically, part of the test was to teach approaching junctions only, then on a separate lesson emerging left and right. It is near impossible to find an area where you can keep turning 'in' or keep turning 'out' emerging from a junction. Instructors can make better use of an area by simply teaching left turns then right turns, and vice versa.

*Manoeuvres you should know
for real driving and the test.*

Manoeuvres can be practiced at almost any time, and often used to break up the driving. It is important to note that some instructors may teach you the manoeuvres early in your training which may make you feel that because you've done all the manoeuvres, you are ready for your driving test, this is often not the case. Some instructors may wait to teach you the manoeuvres at the end of your training. A client centred approach should give you some choice on when you do the manoeuvres but always listen to your instructor's advice.

Once you have mastered junctions, you can then go on to drive in busier areas and master how to negotiate traffic, deal with other road users and start decision making yourself, while getting used to more challenging junctions and roads. We call this, Road Procedure.

Road procedures are the most complex as they often involve the actions of others.

This section of learning to drive can be one of the most challenging ones, as the element of anticipation encompasses most of the above. Anticipation develops with experience.

Each time another road user catches you out, instead of getting annoyed, treat it as education, you will learn more from your mistakes than getting it right all the time.

Making mistakes is not as important as knowing what to do after the mistake has happened and how to rectify it. This needs to carry on forever, remember we have to learn from our mistakes, it's not always the learner driver who makes mistakes either, but all mistakes are lessons in disguise. Any driver on the road can make a mistake, even one that has been driving for many years. As the saying goes, 'to err is human,' and this is absolutely the case in driving. It is how you deal with yours and other people's mistakes without getting annoyed. It all goes towards making you a better driver.

Hopefully, you will only make the mistakes described as lapses or errors, these are the common mistakes that rarely result in a full-blown incident. However, if these mistakes are not recognised by you and your instructor, and not corrected, they will become a habit and can contribute to being involved in an incident. It's not the big things that we do or don't do on the road that matter the most, it's the little things we do or don't do that make the biggest difference.

Other mistakes that can only be described as violations, these are often done deliberately such as, driving well above speed limits or passing through red traffic lights. Driving above the speed limit can also be a lapse of concentration but driving consistently above the speed limit is a violation. Those who simply ignore the rules of the road coupled with a careless attitude are known as 'crash magnets.' These people think rules are meant to be broken.

When we are talking about speed limits, traffic lights, solid white lines etc. It's not just rules we are breaking, it's the law.

During your driving course you should also be given all the important information on how to become a driver who will be skilled for life, it is impossible to experience everything driving throws at you in 40 hours or so on the road, so sometimes this can be done by having a quick discussion during some lessons coupled with handouts, etc.

Some of these discussions can be done on the move, which also helps you get used to driving and talking at the same time.

Discussions can take place at any time, and are an important part of being a well-rounded, skilled driver.

These are not only discussions; they can also be the focus of a driving lesson. For example, if you are coming up to your driving test and your driving is consistently at test standard, instead of stopping your lessons and getting out of practice you can use some of these discussions to use as the focus of a lesson.

Naturally, there will be other things to learn and develop as cars change, rules change, and road norms change. By getting the basics right at the very beginning and learning good habits to be a skilled driver for life, it will be much easier to adapt to the changes to driving as they come along. One of the most important skills you should develop with the help of your instructor is 'anticipation'. You can also do this as a passenger, even on a bus and can second guess what other road users are going to do next. In fact, half a second of anticipation can reduce the likelihood of you being involved in a collision by half.

Structuring a great driving lesson.

This is a typical structure of a great driving lesson, of course this will vary from instructor to instructor, but there should be a beginning, a middle and an end.

The Beginning

The lesson should begin by having a quick chat with the pupil to set the goals for the lesson. At the end of the lesson the learner should come back with a better understanding, skill or simply be better at something, even if the goal has changed throughout the lesson. They don't need to be perfect at the end of the lesson, just better.

· Establish the goals

· The learner must clearly understand what they are doing, and what role or level of help the instructor is going to give.

The lesson could comprise the following:

→ The instructor could talk through instructions as the learner follows them.

→ The instructor could prompt the learner to take responsibility for certain tasks.

→ The instructor could assess the learner as they take full responsibility.

A discussion should take place with the learner regarding the weather (if appropriate), the joint responsibility for the risk and exactly who is doing what.

The start of the lesson

The route should allow situations and junctions to make the goals happen. Your instructor must respond to what is happening in the **actual** lesson, it doesn't matter what the learner has done or not done before; the instructor must deal with whatever needs the learner needs help with and adapt the lesson as required. Learners can do things wrong that they have previously got right. The instructor must adapt to what is happening in the moment. The learner must do things for themselves, for example the instructor should not just keep in control by simply telling the learner everything or constantly grabbing the steering wheel or using the dual controls. This is over-instruction. The instructor must transfer responsibility to the learner so they can make (safe) mistakes. Making mistakes is how we learn and improve our driving.

Another form of over-instruction is to tell the learner driver to do things they should already know how to do. For example, if junctions are the focus of the lessons the instructor should not have to talk to the learner though moving off and stopping. If this is needed, then the lesson needs to change to focus on learning or developing those skills.

The instructor still needs to identify the mistakes, (or 'faults' as the DVSA call them), analyse and rectify them. This ensures the learner is much more involved. The instructor needs to help the learner establish what was wrong; why it went wrong and how to fix it.

It is vital that the instructor watches the learner, and looks for non-verbal communication, answers their questions, and reacts when they exclaim, gasp or use an expletive.

The learner could be nervous and may occasionally make mistakes that the instructor may not be ready for. If this happens the instructor should help the learner to adapt and rectify the mistakes, this makes sure the learner simply learns this skill which hopefully will carry on once they have passed and driving alone. The learner and instructor should be involved in the decision making. The instructor should say. 'How about we fix this or try this, does this sound like a plan?' Mistakes should not go unnoticed but discussed.

If you need to pull over to discuss things at length then do so, fixing mistakes on the move is fine if the learner has forgotten, but if it keeps happening, then again pull over to discuss. If the mistake is due to lack of knowledge or serious enough to fail a test, then again, pull over to discuss.

The end of the lesson

The end of the lesson should include a recap, including what went well, what they could have improved on and how the instructor could have offered the learner driver any more help or done something different to help them reach the goals.

The learner has to come back improved, and if this means improved on the mistakes that went on, it does not mean they have to have improved on the original goal that was set but to have understood what they did right or wrong and how they could improve in the next lesson. After all, this is what they are paying for.

How should you structure your lessons, once a week or as an intensive course?

The only answer to this is do what suits you, you as an individual learner and as a person. Some instructors or driving schools will sell you an intensive course, primarily because that's what suits them. Make sure you decide what suits you and don't be coerced into multiple hour lessons or lessons every day if it isn't suitable for you.

Traditionally, learning to drive was a one-hour lesson per week. Doing one lesson for an hour per week could take you longer to learn to drive and end up costing you more. In the past more learners undertook private practice with their mum, dad or an older sibling which cut the hours down with a professional instructor, but many people don't seem to do this now. This can be because they either don't have the time or cannot get insurance for the learner to drive their car. Traffic patterns and volume of traffic has changed so much, not to mention the driving test, plus the level of skill and ability that is required to pass the modern test today. The number of driving lessons mainly depends now on your ability to retain information and skill, coupled with the teaching and coaching ability of your instructor.

On the other end of the scale, there are intensive courses where you are expected to cram 40 hours of tuition into one week and take your driving test at the end of that week. This can get you your licence quicker, and it is possible to pass your driving test this way. However, the retention of knowledge and skills can diminish quickly after your test pass, with disastrous results.

Many learners who have passed their driving test this way often report that they can't remember much about their lessons or they feel very nervous when driving on their own, especially on roads they don't know.

For intensive courses to work you will have to concentrate on passing your driving test rather than learning to drive safely for life or how to self-analyse and self-correct your mistakes. There are drivers on the roads who have been driving for years, yet still make mistakes. What chance has someone got with about 40 hours of practice covering around 500 miles of getting it right all the time, and trying to remember what they learnt a few weeks ago during that intense and stressful week? It must be a bit like trying to remember a shopping list you made out and lost last month!

There may be no turning back once the course is booked, with the driving test booked at the end of the week. There is little time to change or cancel should anything go wrong. So, if you have paid for the full course and something happens where you need to cancel the course it could be impossible to get your money back. There are lots of reasons people suspend their driving lessons, and this could be you. Also, beware of courses that book your practical driving test, even before you have passed your theory test. I have heard that some companies book the test in someone else's name, then swap it to your name once you have passed your theory test. Some of these tests are booked in an area that you may have never driven in or will take your lessons in. I have been told by someone this happened to them. The company they used for their lessons just told them they will book a test, but never told them it would not be their local test centre or the test centre in the location they have been learning in, so you could be taking your driving test anywhere.

While the area you take your test in shouldn't make a difference, because if you have the skills and knowledge that have to be in place for you to stay safe and skilled on the roads you should be able to drive on any road well. In reality, you can still feel uncomfortable and lose a lot of confidence which can make the difference between a test pass or a test fail.

Taken at face value it could be a good thing to get it all over and done with quickly as you can pass your driving test by the end of the week. However, when does the real learning take place? Any excellent teacher will tell you that learning to be permanent, the knowledge and the skill has to be stored in the long-term memory not the short-term memory.

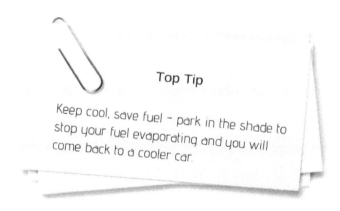

Top Tip

Keep cool, save fuel – park in the shade to stop your fuel evaporating and you will come back to a cooler car.

The reflective stage of learning where knowledge is transferred from short to long-term memory, is where the real learning is done. This usually happens while the brain is relaxed, and during an intensive driving course this rarely happens. After all, how many people can remember a long shopping list when they have forgotten to take it with them? It is easy to remember the things we need every day, for example bread and milk, but what about the ingredients for a recipe?

What *is* the best way then? In my experience 1.5 hours every other day or so, spread over a few weeks is the optimum way of learning to drive, if this suits your learning style and of course your budget. This gives the learner time to relax and reflect between lessons and time to get in some private practice, either behind the wheel or as a passenger. The more situations you encounter and deal with and the more miles you cover before taking your driving test the more likely you are to not only pass the test for the first time but become a skilled driver for life.

Doing an intensive course can be stressful. I can remember my own experiences in trying to do intensive courses. At the time I was a new instructor, and they advised me that this was the best way. I started the lessons on Monday with the test booked for Friday afternoon, and in those days, you had to give 10 working days' notice to change or cancel a driving test. So, when things did not go to plan, either my pupil or I would be in tears by Wednesday. If you are driving four to six hours per day while learning to drive, the last thing you want to do is get in a car with someone and do more. This amount of daily driving is, even for an experienced driver, exhausting enough without the learning process added to the mix. Once the intensive course is over, it is important that you feel confident when you pass your driving test as your licence allows you to drive for life on any road, in any weather, with anyone or on your own.

Having said all of this, there are outside influences that can dictate how you do a course. For example, someone might need a driving licence really quickly for a new job. Just remember you will learn to pass a test. You might believe that learning to drive and passing your driving test are the same thing. Unfortunately, they are not, if you are learning with an instructor who is just teaching you to pass your test and keeping you on test routes, then you are being short-changed. I heard a statistic that about 40% of new drivers are not confident driving on their own once they have passed their driving test. Many of them still cannot park or navigate for themselves. If this is true, it really does prove that it's vital to learn how to drive safely for life, and not just learn how to pass your driving test.

Key point to remember...

We all learn at our own pace and you should not compare what you are doing with your friends. Although your friend might be up to roundabouts and you are only up to left turns, it does NOT follow that your friend is learning faster. They might be up to roundabouts, but how good are they?

If you are thinking about getting some private practice between your driving lessons with your instructor, there are some insurance companies who will insure a learner driver for a few weeks at a time, and it can be very cost effective. If you and a supervising driver have time and a car available that will allow you to get some private practice in, I would recommend you do it. You and your instructor will know when you get to the skill level that will allow you to do this in relative safety. Beware, sometimes private practice lessons with a partner or parent can result in arguments which may be counterproductive. Always practice the techniques your instructor is teaching you and not the 'old-fashioned' way of driving. The last thing you want to do is copy someone's bad habits. Remember, that any person who sits with you on your practice driving lessons must be a full driving licence holder in the category of vehicle they are supervising you in, they must have held that licence for over 3.5 years and be over 21 years of age. There are also some hire companies that will hire dual control cars by the hour.

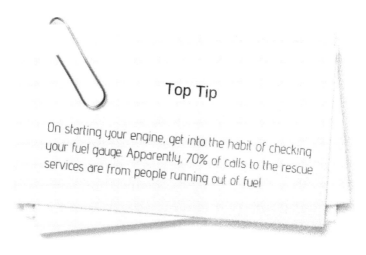

Top Tip

On starting your engine, get into the habit of checking your fuel gauge. Apparently, 70% of calls to the rescue services are from people running out of fuel.

If funding your lessons is an issue, it is best to save up enough money to do a full course of lessons, even if it's just once a week or a semi-intensive course. Some driving schools will offer you a discount if you buy 10 lessons or more in one go, they call it a block booking. Remember to read the small print regarding refunds (some courses have to be paid in full and are not refundable) also, check when you can take the lessons and make sure you get a receipt and get each lesson signed for. If you pay an instructor directly for your lessons, even if they are with a franchise, then the contract is between you and that driving instructor not with the driving school, so any refunds will have to come from that individual instructor.

If you pay the driving school the money directly, then the contract is between you and the driving school. Professional driving schools ring fence your money and keep it in a separate bank account, sometimes known as a client's account, and it will only be released once each lesson has taken place and that the learner is happy with the lesson. Some independent driving instructors may also do this for you. A few driving schools even ask you to sign to release the money to the driving instructor. If you get halfway through the lessons and change your mind, or stop lessons, or you just want to change instructors, then it should be easy to do, if you have paid the driving school then you can swap instructors without the hassle of asking for a refund.

If you change your instructor, this should not mean you have to start all over again with your lessons. A good instructor will assess you on your first lesson with them, this could mean assessing you from the beginning by driving to a location where you can get comfortable with them and their car, they will then ask you to move off and stop, if all goes well, they will continue to add more complex driving tasks and junctions and just fill in the gaps when and if needed.

If you have any concerns regarding your instructor's behaviour or how they are teaching you, speak to your instructor. You are paying them; they are not like a teacher in school that you don't have any choice about. You should not be afraid to talk to your instructor about your concerns, however, if you would rather speak to the driving school you can do this too, that is, if they are part of a multi-car driving school.

If all else fails and your concern is serious enough, then report your instructor to the DVSA. I have provided a link in Appendix 9 that takes you through the steps.

A young lady phoned to make an appointment for her first driving lesson. I asked if she had her provisional licence and could she bring it with her, to which she said she would. On picking her up, I drove to a quiet corner of an industrial estate and chatted with her to gain some information on her; had she ever driven before, was she at work or still at school, etc. Once we had arrived at my chosen spot, I asked for her licence.

"Oh, it hasn't arrived yet," she said.

I explained that I had asked her on the telephone to bring it along... So as not to lose a lesson, I said that I could cover the first lesson on a side road, which although tarmacked, didn't lead anywhere.

I explained that I could cover most of what was needed, but without her licence, I couldn't allow her behind the wheel. She understood and at the end of the lesson I prompted her to chase up her licence as they are normally quick to arrive and I couldn't understand why hers hadn't.

The next week, I picked her up again for her pre-arranged lesson. She still had no provisional driving licence, so a repeat of last weeks' lesson - lots of demos and explanations, but no actual driving. I took her home and once again, spoke about my concern that she had yet to receive it and asked her when exactly did she apply for it.

She then told me that her mum said she couldn't apply for it until the end of the month when it would be cheaper to buy!

I didn't see her again.

Barbara Trafford – ADI Federation

Chapter 6

Your Theory Test

Did you know prior to July 1996 there was no theory test?

Passing your theory test is the first step in gaining a full driving licence. My daughter Emily opened up a whole new way of thinking for me, not long after she turned 17.

Emily commented many times on the Driving Theory Test questions, 'that's a stupid question' or 'why do I have to know that to drive safely?' I must admit that I agreed with her, especially regarding the first aid questions. I strongly believe that first aid should be taught in schools. Why wait until people are learning to drive to teach these important lifesaving lessons? Not everyone will learn to drive. In the 30-plus years I have been driving, I have never seen a crash, I have never been in a situation when I have had to get out of my car and help someone with any sort of first aid. So, I can't understand why the DVSA has put so much emphasis in the theory test on first aid. In my opinion if we want to teach young people first aid it should be within the school curriculum and not on the driving theory test.

Anyway, back to the theory test, many of us remember the days when you simply had to answer a few highway code questions, asked by the examiner at the end of the driving test. Today, there are up to 50 questions, some of which are about first aid, others are about dealing with crashes, motorway driving and even driver attitude.

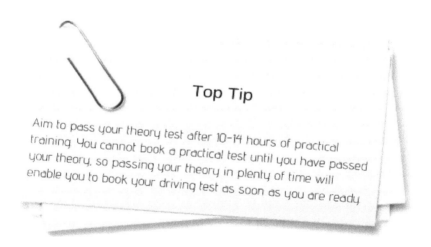

Top Tip

Aim to pass your theory test after 10-14 hours of practical training. You cannot book a practical test until you have passed your theory, so passing your theory in plenty of time will enable you to book your driving test as soon as you are ready

It is vital that you are fully prepared for your theory test. Not only will it help you pass this test the first time it will also give you a good grounding of the rules, laws and regulations of the road. The theory test is not just about what the signs or road markings mean or what you should and shouldn't do on the road it is also about attitude and behaviour and as you will read in this book having a good attitude on the road is the foundation of a competent driver.

When taking your practical driving test or driving on your own, it is vital that you have a good understanding of the rules of the road and what best practise is. If you choose just to rote learn the questions, just give it a go or pass on a guess then it is highly likely you will let yourself down on your practical driving test, you could even end up with penalty points or going to court for not knowing a rule or a law that you should have known, lack of knowledge is no defence when you are faced with the long arm of the law.

There are many ways to practise for your theory test. Choose the best way that suits you and your learning style. Some driving schools and instructors will help you to study for this test, by offering one-to-one theory lessons. There are also various apps and online training you can do. I have mentioned some of these in Appendix 9. You might find once you begin studying that you actually know more than you thought you knew. The best way is to do some practise questions and research the questions you have either guessed, got wrong or you do not know, so you are studying things you do not know instead of going over the same things time and time again or reading the whole Highway Code cover to cover. I don't even think I could do that.

As it stands, there are four possible answers to each question, so there is a 25% chance of getting a question correct, even with a guess! Which could mean that some learners may simply go to take the theory test without studying enough or studying at all.

I can remember when the questions for the theory test were first introduced, many driving instructors thought that it would be great to run proper theory test sessions in a classroom. However, the DVSA in their wisdom just published all the questions with all the answers, which may have led to some people passing purely using rote learning with no real understanding or underpinning knowledge.

There is a question book of over 700 questions, which are widely available in many formats, from paperback books, DVD's to phone apps. Some learners will study the questions or memorise the answers, but the most important thing is knowing why the answer is the answer. This will really underpin the knowledge and understanding needed not only to stay safe but to keep out of trouble. It is amazing how many drivers lose their licence because they simply don't know all the rules.

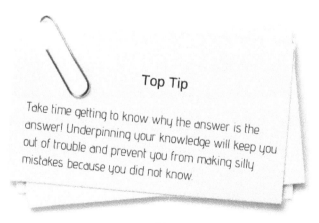

Top Tip

Take time getting to know why the answer is the answer! Underpinning your knowledge will keep you out of trouble and prevent you from making silly mistakes because you did not know.

Using multi-response answers would have been much more in tune to real-world driving, where there is often more than one correct answer. The multi-response question requires thorough learning rather than remembering a list of pre-approved answers from the published DVSA question bank.

This would have made sure that learners had to study properly and gain a better understanding of the theory behind the practical driving skill. Also, they could attend structured theory training, either on a one-to-one basis, in a classroom or a workshop setting. Attending classroom theory lessons is a common practice in some European countries. This would allow new drivers to gain a real understanding and be able to challenge the wrong type of knowledge often gained from parents or friends, more of this in the fact and fiction section.

I encounter lots of incorrectly learnt rules of the road. For instance, in 2005, I had been delivering the police diversionary courses, and I had met many experienced drivers that really believed once they passed their driving test it's perfectly acceptable to break or bend the 'rules' as they refer to them, but as we know they are not rules they are actually laws, the minority of people actually feel they should be allowed to get away with it too. These laws are in place to keep us all safe from injury or even death. In fact, the Highway Code could be considered as a document of people's past mistakes, if there many crashes because people were driving in yellow flip-flops, it would be put in the Highway Code, that you should not drive in yellow flip-flops.

Here is an example of someone who thought they should be able to break the rules. An advanced driver who I won't name and shame, had a huge rant on Facebook when I had put a post-up about Speed Cameras, it was an article on how to not get caught speeding, it simply stated 'don't speed, then you won't get caught', I had put it up hopefully to raise a smile or two. The man took umbrage because he had been caught speeding doing 36mph on a 30mph road. He said he had good observation, he had risk-assessed the road for himself and he decided because of all of this and the fact he has passed an advanced driving test, that it was perfectly acceptable for him to do 36mph in a 30mph zone on that road. He chose to break the speed limit, it was not a simple mistake or a lapse of concentration, he did it on purpose. He also stated it was late at night, too. I wanted to point out that if his observations were so great, he should have seen the camera, but as he did not see the humour of the article, I doubted he would have taken that comment well. As an advanced driver he should have known that more people are killed and seriously injured late at night or early in the morning, he simply should have been more respectful, and not thought that just because he was an advanced driver he was above the law, apologies, I have gone off on a tangent again, so let's get back to the theory test.

To pass the theory test, learners have to answer 43 out of 50 questions correctly, and all the questions are multiple choice.

The second part of the theory test is the hazard perception test. You will be required to watch 14 video clips of up to one-minute long each. 13 of the clips will have one scoring hazard in them and one clip will have two scoring hazards in it. To pass you have to get a score of 57 out of a possible 75. During the test, you just have to click the computer mouse when you see a developing hazard. Note the word developing.

A scoring window will open at a specific place in the video, if you click the mouse as soon as the window opens, you will score five on that clip. Each moment you wait to identify the developing hazard correctly, you will cause the score to drop from five to four to three to two to one to zero.

The important thing to remember is if you click outside the scoring window before it opens or starts, you will still score zero. If you click after the scoring window closes, you will also score a zero. I feel that when the program was written, the score of one would mean in the real world of driving, that you would be too late to react to the hazard safely but scoring a five also doesn't mean that you will be great on the road. I think this test lends itself to game playing, as all it shows is that people can spot developing hazards. What it doesn't show is if that person could deal with those developing hazards in the real world. Think about it, just because you can spot potential danger while watching a film, it does not mean that you will do this effectively while driving, or in fact, know what to do about the danger when you see it. But it's a start, and perhaps it shows people the theory about hazards. However, research conducted in Great Britain and Australia does show a link between scoring high on the hazard perception test and the new drivers having fewer collisions or crashes. I have added the links to this research in Appendix 9. There could be multiple potential hazards of all kinds in the clips, however, the scoring hazards are the hazards that are the developing hazards. For example, hazards which are developing into something dangerous or potentially dangerous, you can click on the clips as many times as you wish, but you will not score extra for spotting other hazards and dangers. In fact, if you click rhythmically or too many times the system thinks you are cheating and you will score zero for the clip; if this happens a red X will come up to tell you this clip has scored zero.

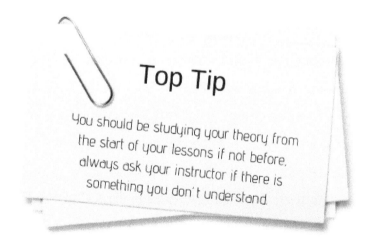

Top Tip

You should be studying your theory from the start of your lessons if not before, always ask your instructor if there is something you don't understand

One way to ensure you have the best possible chance of passing is to first relax. It's also advantageous to hold the mouse in your hand, not on the table and sit back from the screen a little as it's easier to see the developing hazards this way.

You will have already done the multiple-choice questions before you start the hazard perception part of the test, so don't rush into it.

Once those questions are finished you will be given a chance to review your answers. If you have finished the questions with plenty of time, do not click 'end test' immediately as this starts a one-minute countdown to the hazard perception part. As you will have already been staring at a computer screen for quite a while, your eyes could probably do with a rest. So, if you have some time left, use it to give your eyes a rest or even close them. Don't fall asleep though because once your time is up on the multiple-choice; the hazard perception part of the test starts automatically.

If you have time and you have rested your eyes, simply press 'end test to start the hazard perception part.'

Anecdotally, drivers with experience on the road often fail the hazard perception test because they are clicking on the hazard too early, or they might not agree that the 'scoring' hazard is even a hazard. As you can imagine, a driver who has been driving many years and has had no one pull out in front of them from a side road, may not consider that a car travelling towards the end of the side road a hazard, versus another driver who had someone pull out of a side road in front of them causing them to have a near miss, they will see cars coming to the end of the side road as a major hazard.

If during your practice, you find you are clicking too early, give this strategy a go. As soon as you notice the 'scoring' hazard click the mouse, then click again; so, if you clicked just before the scoring window, the second click will register your score. If you score five on your first click and three on your second click the system will pick up your maximum score, so you don't have to worry about clicking twice. Please don't click over two to three times per hazard, remember the system may detect rhythmic clicking.

It is worth mentioning again that one clip will have two developing hazards in it, so keep watching all the clips to the end so you are ready for the second hazard. From the 28th September 2020, the theory test included three multiple-choice questions based on a short video that you have watched.

The theory test can only be taken in English or Welsh and it can be signed for deaf or hard-of-hearing students.

You can have extra time if you have a reading or a writing challenge, such as dyslexia and a voice-over in either English or Welsh. However, you must declare anything you need help with when you book the test, as this cannot be arranged on the day of the test.

You must take your UK photo card driving licence to your test. During the COVID-19 Pandemic in 2020/1 you also had to wear a face covering, unless there is a good reason why you could not wear one, wearing glasses did not count as a good reason. You also had to say why you could not wear a face covering when you booked your test. If you did not, and you turned up to your test without a face covering, your test was cancelled.

Try to arrive around 10 minutes before your appointment time, this will allow you time to find the test centre, if you have not done a 'dry run' already and if you smoke, time for that too. You will not be allowed to take anyone into the test centre with you, there is no waiting area, so if you are being dropped off, the person with you will have to find somewhere else to wait.

When you get to reception your appointment time and identification will be checked. You will then need to sign a digital display, then you are appointed a locker for your belongings and hand the key. You will not be allowed to take anything into the testing room with you. Your mobile phone must be switched off before you put it in the locker, and you must inform the official on reception that you had done this. You will then be asked to read the rules document before you are taken to the test room and assigned a computer station.

You will then see some general information on the theory test, reminding you on how many questions and time you will be allocated. You will have an option to do five practise questions, just to help you get into the swing of things and give you a bit of time to relax.

Remember, you can flag questions which will allow you to go back to, if there is time, and double check your answers, please don't flag them all or keep second guessing yourself. Once you hit the end test button, the hazard perception test will start, again you will see some general information and have some practise clips to do. After each clip there is a countdown of 10 seconds before the next clip starts.

At the end of the test, you have an option to answer some feedback questions from the DVSA.

Once you have finished your test you need to get up quietly to go back to the reception desk. Before you can receive your results, your identification is checked again, you can at this point collect your belongings from your locker and hand back the key. You will be called back to the reception desk once your results are ready.

Remember your theory pass certificate is only valid for two years from the date you passed. You must take and pass your practical driving test within those two years. During the Covid-19 pandemic many learner drivers had their theory pass certificates expire. There was a big push from the driving instructor industry and members of the public to have the certificates extended. After a long battle with the government, they decided not to extend them. The reason given by the government was that they wanted all new drivers to have the most up to date knowledge of the rules of the road, legislation and law before passing a practical driving test, this was in order to keep our roads safe.

I feel this was a massive disservice to all learner drivers, if this was the case then all drivers should have this up-to-date knowledge, we should all be tested every two years at theory level. I won't repeat the number of drivers who have been driving for many years, yet simply do not know the rules and regulations. If the government was serious about road safety, they would introduce regular refresher courses for all drivers and riders.

In late 1989 as part of a national competition, sponsored by Volvo and regional newspapers across the UK, I was successful in completing several theory and practical elements of a competition to become 'West Midlands Safe Driver of the Year'. My prize involved an all-expenses-paid 11-day motoring holiday in Sweden, with spending money and an invite to a presentation dinner at the Volvo plant in Gothenburg. The following Spring, we travelled across to Sweden on the overnight ferry with my wife and 18-month-old son in my driving school Metro. We arrived in Sweden and made our way to our log cabin in a forest area south of Gothenburg – excellent. Having unloaded the car and a quick refresh we decided to go for a short drive to explore the local area. Within a few miles, my drive came to an abrupt stop as I encountered a moose emerging from the woods at the side of the road. Metro versus moose… there was only ever going to be one winner. The front of the Metro took the force of the impact leaving the bonnet and radiator grill looking the worse for wear. The radiator itself was punctured and (subsequently discovering that there was not one Austin Rover dealership in Sweden) I had to rely on improvisation by using rad-weld and chewing gum in an attempt to stem the leaks for the rest of the holiday.

The day came when we were to attend the awards dinner at the Volvo plant, I had been given a letter of introduction (in Swedish) that I was to give to the staff at the security gatehouse. On arrival, I gave the letter to the uniformed security guard on duty, which I am assuming made reference to the fact that I was the 'Safe Driver of the Year'. On reading the letter, he slowly walked to the front of my Metro, smiled and then beckoned to his colleagues to come out and have a look. I'm not sure of exactly what was being said between them, but I got the impression that they found a certain degree of humour in my status as 'Safe Driver of the Year'.

Alan Prosser – Telford

Chapter 7

Your Practical Test

Why is taking a driving test so stressful?

My indication that a pupil was ready for the test is whether I would lend them my own car. If this person needed my car in an emergency would I happily hand them my car keys? If the answer was yes, then I knew they were ready to pass their practical driving test.

Passing your practical driving test is just the start of the journey, if you feel confident to drive completely on your own then you will be confident in taking your driving test.

TASK: Ask yourself the following questions -

- Do I feel confident driving on roads I do not know?
- Do I feel confident following the SatNav to somewhere I have not been before?
- Do I feel confident giving a lift to one of my younger siblings or perhaps a friend's child?

If you feel confident to take on this responsibility, the chances are you may be ready for your driving test.

The following questions were compiled by one of the Insight 2 Drive instructors who became an examiner.

TASK: Answer these questions honestly:

1. Can you operate all the controls, when required, with no prompting? This includes gears, handbrake, indicators and windscreen wipers amongst others.

A) Yes.

B) Most of the time.

C) No, I still need instruction from my driving instructor.

2. Can you cope with every situation you meet in your driving lessons, including rural roads, dual carriageways, roundabouts, town traffic, etc?

A) Yes.

B) Most situations, but the odd thing still worries me.

C) No, I still need instruction from my driving instructor.

3. Does your driving instructor ever need to reach across and use any of the controls to keep you and the car safe?

A) No, not anymore.

B) Occasionally.

C) In most driving lessons.

4. Can you complete all the manoeuvres with no prompting and with full observations?

A) Yes.

B) Usually, but I still occasionally clip the kerb or end up wide.

c) I still find manoeuvres difficult.

5. Do you feel that you sometimes hold up the traffic behind you?

A) No, I keep up with the traffic flow, but without breaking the speed limit.

B) Sometimes I still stall or seem to take a while to get up to speed.

C) I feel like traffic seems to get frustrated with me, and sometimes people try to overtake me.

6. Are you comfortable driving at 60 or 70 mph, in traffic?

A) Yes, and I am happy to overtake when necessary.

B) Usually, but I'm still a little nervous of overtaking.

C) I'm still not happy at these speeds.

If you have answered all 'A's, then you are probably ready to take your driving test.

If there are one or maybe two 'B's in there, ask your driving instructor about booking the driving test. The waiting lists can be six or seven weeks in some driving test centres, so there will be plenty of time to improve before your driving test, after the lockdowns of 2020/1 the waiting times were months not weeks.

If there are more than two 'B's or any 'C's, then you are not quite ready to take your practical driving test yet.

Get ready for your driving test - the importance of mock tests.

The DVSA strongly advises you to do a mock test before your actual driving test. The benefits of a mock test are that you will be better prepared for the actual driving test. You will now have an idea on what it is like to drive for around 40 minutes without the instructor helping you or asking any questions. It is my opinion that a mock test should be conducted by another driving instructor, if you are learning with a multi-car driving school this should be very easy to arrange, if you're not, it can still be arranged. In my local area lots of instructors, even though they are technically competitors they still help each other out and are always there for each other.

Conducting a mock test correctly can highlight any weaknesses you may have, so your lessons leading up to the real test can be focused on those weaknesses. It can also help you understand the whole testing process and get you mentally prepared for the actual driving test, if time allows it can be a good idea to just visit the test centre and if possible, to go in, this will take away any fear you have on what the waiting room, car park, toilets are like, this was not possible just after the 2020/1 national and local lockdowns as restrictions were still in place.

According to the DVSA, doing a mock test can increase your chances of a first-time pass, which can only have a positive effect on waiting times. This was especially important when the impact of COVID-19 increased the waiting times for driving tests immeasurably.

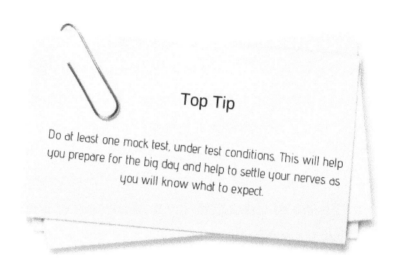

Top Tip

Do at least one mock test, under test conditions. This will help you prepare for the big day and help to settle your nerves as you will know what to expect.

It can also be a lot cheaper to do a mock test with another instructor rather than 'chance it' with the real thing. Most driving instructors charge for at least two hours on the test day and you will have to pay the test fee too, which is currently £62.00. A mock test should cost you no more than a normal lesson fee.

Mock tests can also benefit the driving instructor as it can encourage them to self-reflect on their own competence and if the instructor conducting the mock test finds a weakness, it can help them to improve too. For example, if the pupil fails and insists they did not know something or were told something was okay, the instructor can now change the way they teach that something or explain it in a different way. Mock tests can lead to a greater first-time pass rate for the driving instructor, this will help them gain a fantastic reputation, especially if this is coupled with great coaching techniques and helping someone improve their skills and knowledge in order to drive safely and skillfully for life. I must stress at this point having a first-time pass rate based solely on sticking to test routes and teaching someone to just pass a test, is a reputation I would not like.

Having said all this, it is no use doing lots of mock tests, one or two should suffice, doing multiple tests will eat away at your training time and make you feel the test is something so different and challenging that you may feel that you must practise the test to pass it, all you have to do is practice safe and skilled driving. I will give you more information about mock tests later in the book, when we go through some driving test myths.

Most people have some nerves on the day of their driving test, this is completely natural. It doesn't mean that because you are nervous you are not ready. When my daughter went for her driving test, she was extremely nervous, bearing in mind her driving instructor was also her mother, and we had covered many miles. I think it was more to do with not letting me down than her driving skills. I accompanied her for months while driving, which you could say was private practise, I knew she had all the skills and ability to drive solo and therefore, easily pass her driving test.

When you are facing possibly something you have never faced before, it is natural to be nervous, or if you have taken a test before and failed then you know the outcome can be a negative one, so your link back to those feelings you felt when you failed the first time, this can intensify the feeling of nervousness the more test fails behind us the more intense the feeling of nervousness can be, and you will bring past emotions onto the current situation.

What is the best way to deal with test nerves?

There are many ways of dealing with test nerves and the best one is the one that works for you. I'll explore as many as I can but I'm sure there are many more so please listen to your instructors suggestions and try as many as you can, to see if they work for you.

One of the things that helps me is remembering a conversation I had with a gentleman called John Farlam, I'm sure most instructors who may read this book will have heard the name John Farlam before. I did a week's training with John back in 2005. Many years later I was delivering a presentation at the ADINJC National Conference, as this was the first time I had presented in front of a large group of my respected peers, I was very nervous. After a quick chat with John my nerves simply went, he asked me how I was feeling, physically. I replied I felt short of breath, my heart was racing, and my stomach was turning. John simply said, 'oh that sounds like you're excited, not nervous' and he told me there is a very fine line between being nervous and being excited, the physical attributes are very similar, we just have to decide which one we want to be. So, are you nervous about taking your driving test or are you excited with the prospect of getting your licence and your freedom? On the day of your test ask yourself are the feelings really nerves or are they excitement? I chose excitement on that day and my presentation went down really well. I think!

Another way people deal with test nerves is breathing. Yes, I know we all do it naturally, but if you use circular breathing, which is in through the nose and out through the mouth, in through the nose and out through the mouth, concentrate on your breathing for a couple of minutes this should calm you down, please do not concentrate too much on your breathing while driving though. Another way to change your breathing is to take a deep breath in quickly and a long breath out slowly this will help you relax, this technique is often used to help people fall asleep, in fact it is what we do naturally when falling asleep, it relaxes the mind and the body, ready for a good night's sleep, do not try this one when driving. Listening to music might help you relax, either slow, soothing music or your favourite upbeat tune, again whatever works for you.

Thought Field Therapy

Diane Hall of 'L of a way to Pass' explains, some learner drivers really enjoy learning to drive and even look forward to their driving test, but many learners experience driving test nerves and even driving anxiety. There are a range of psychological techniques that you can use to enable you to control your emotions, rather than your emotions controlling you, ensuring that you can remain calm, focused, and confident on not only your driving lessons but also your driving test. One technique is called Thought Field Therapy (TFT). This is so effective that it has been used on soldiers who experience P.T.S.D. Diane Hall is a driving instructor and therapist, and she specialises in helping people with driving anxiety and test nerves and recommends using TFT alongside other techniques. Diane says that TFT is incredibly effective, can be done in minutes, and can be used for a range of issues from driving anxiety, through to test nerves, panic at busy junctions, or feeling intimidated by other road users. If you would like to learn more about this technique, I have included a link to Diane's website in Appendix 9.

Nearly everybody is nervous about their driving test so don't feel that you are alone in this. Today, driving test examiners are aware of how nervous people can get and are far more friendly now than they ever have been, and they will do their best to make you feel at ease.

Mindfulness

Kev & Tracey Field of Confident Drivers say mindfulness and learning to drive may not be two activities that you naturally think fit together, as most people imagine mindfulness as being only about meditation. However, some simple mindfulness exercises can help manage driving anxiety and nerves by keeping you in the present moment. Mindfulness is simply being aware of what you are sensing and feeling in the moment, without interpretation or judgement.

This includes;

- What is happening around you
- Your senses - sight, sound, smell, taste, touch
- Physical sensations in your body
- Your emotions, moods, attitude

Practising being mindful will help you improve your focus and attention on your driving. You may already have experienced being focused and aware while concentrating on a driving lesson. You may also have experienced driving lessons when your attention is anywhere but on the road. Most people would agree that they would like other drivers on the road to be in the present moment, being aware of what is happening around them while driving.

Often, we spend time with a narrow focus, paying attention to what is going on in our minds, thoughts, feelings, worries, memories, daydreams, and things that might happen in the future. The problem with spending so much time in an inner world of thought, especially while driving, is that not only are we distracted, it also creates fear, doubt and anxiety.

Driving anxiety and nerves are often a fear of what **might** happen rather than what is happening in the present moment.

If you feel anxious before driving, concentrating on what is happening in the moment can help interrupt feelings of anxiety.

If you feel anxious while driving, focusing on the actions of driving in the present moment and describing what is happening aloud, can be less anxiety provoking and is an example of how being mindful doesn't have to involve meditation.

If you feel distracted or anxious and are parked at the side of the road, you can try this quick mindfulness exercise to reset your attention and bring yourself into the present moment.

- Pause for a moment
- Pay attention to your breathing
- Notice what you can see
- Notice what you can hear
- Notice what you can smell or taste
- Notice fastening your seatbelt (the sounds and sensations)
- Notice the sensation of holding the steering wheel

This quick exercise will help to bring your attention back to the present moment, in the car, ready to continue or start your driving lesson. The Confident Drivers website address is in Appendix 9.

Documents You Must Take To Your Driving Test

- Your UK Driving Licence
- Your Theory Test Pass Certificate (if you have one)
- A Car
- During Covid-19 Pandemic, you also had to bring a face covering, unless you have a good reason not to wear one.

Most people take their test in their instructor's car, the car they've probably driven the most and the car that has dual controls which should keep them and the examiner safe if things go drastically wrong.

You can take your driving test in your own car, if you have one, but it must be insured for the driving test, so please check all your documents before making this decision. Some people feel better taking the test in their own car, so speak to your driving instructor and please take their advice on this. Your driving instructor may not be able to drive your car home after the test as they may not be insured. You may not be insured either as your insurance is for you learning to drive and supervised, so do check your policy. Your instructor should be insured to give you driving lessons in your car.

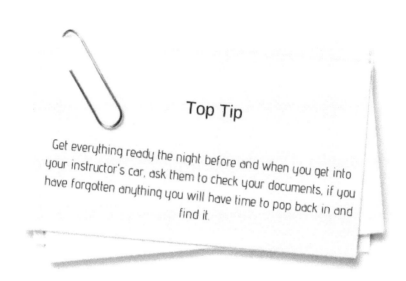

Top Tip

Get everything ready the night before and when you get into your instructor's car, ask them to check your documents, if you have forgotten anything you will have time to pop back in and find it.

On the day of the test, your driving instructor should pick you up with plenty of time to have a quick warm-up drive, check you have all the correct documents and get to the test centre approximately 10 minutes before your test start time. If there is a toilet available you can use it and use the rest of the time to relax and practice your breathing techniques. This is not the time to look at the Highway Code or have discussions on when to signal or not to signal, it is too late now, so relax.

Your driving instructor can even drive you to the test centre and park the car for you, it doesn't have to be you doing all of that.

What is the best day to take your test?

Pick a time of day you know you are at your best, for example if you're not a morning person then don't book the early test time, if you are bright and alert in the early mornings, then do book the early test time. If you want to do an evening or weekend test it usually costs you more. I would always take your instructor's guidance on this and you will find some more information on this in the myths section.

The driving examiner will come into the waiting room, and call your name, I feel it is good manners to stand up and greet the examiner, they will then ask to see your licence, ask you to sign the test sheet (DL25) to confirm that you have the correct car insurance and if you are exempt from wearing a seat belt. They will ask you if you want your driving instructor to come along with you on your test or listen to the debrief at the end of the test.

The 5 Parts To The Driving Test

- An eyesight check
- 'Show me, tell me' safety questions
- Your Driving ability
- Reversing your vehicle
- Independent Driving

The test is the same for both manual and automatic cars

You will then go outside and take an eyesight test, you should be able to read a vehicle number plate with letters 79.4 mm (3.1 inches) high at a minimum distance of 20 metres (about 67 feet), this should be done in good daylight. If you need glasses or contact lenses to read the number plate, then you should always wear them when driving. The 'show me, tell me' vehicle safety questions will be next. One 'tell me' question (where you just explain how you would carry out the task) at the start of your test, before you even start driving and one 'show me' question (where you actually show how you would carry out the task) while you're driving.

You'll get one driving fault (sometimes called a 'minor') if you get one or both questions wrong. The full set of 'show me, tell me' questions and answers can be found in the Appendix 5.

The difference between show and tell is in the name. If the examiner asked you to tell him/her something, you simply have to give a verbal answer, for example, 'tell me how you would check your tyre pressures and where do you find the information on how much air should be in them'. You do not actually check the pressures; you just tell the examiner what you would do.

If the examiner says, 'show me' then you have to do something; for example, 'show me how you would check your headlamps are working' you would then have to switch the lights on and check them. The examiner may ask you about something under the bonnet, you will have to open the bonnet and point to the item. Make sure you remember how to open the bonnet. If your instructor has changed the car, go through this before your test day.

It is also a good idea to check that all the lights are working in the hour before the test and go through all the checks because if you find a fault with the lights, tyres etc. you should have time to get them fixed. After all, bulbs can fail anytime. If it becomes apparent that a bulb, for example, a headlamp bulb is not working at the start of the test, the test will not continue even if it is bright sunlight. If you are using your own car, always check everything is working before you go for your driving test. You might wonder why the 'show me' 'tell me' has been added to the driving test. Simply put, it is to make sure new drivers know both how to, and what to check regularly on their car, so they can maintain the roadworthiness of the car. Once the car is moving you will drive for around 40 minutes.

If you're taking an extended driving test because you've been banned from driving and ordered by a magistrates' court to take the extended test it will be 70 minutes. On all tests you will drive on various roads and in various traffic conditions, but not on motorways, however 70mph national speed limit roads may be included.

The examiner will give you directions for you to follow. Official driving test routes are not published, so you cannot check them before your test, however instructors can memorise some of them and they are often shared with others or even published on websites etc, but they are subject to change and there can be numerous routes from one test centre, so please do not rely on this. You will also be asked to pull over and move away from the side of the road during your test, which can be normal stops at the left-hand side of the road or pulling out from behind a parked vehicle, sometimes called an angled start, you may also be asked to do a hill start. Approximately 30% of test candidates are asked to carry out an emergency or controlled stop. The reversing element or manoeuvres for the test have changed dramatically since I passed my test, to reflect modern driving.

You will be asked to do one of the following exercises

- Parallel park at the side of the road
- Park in a parking bay, either by driving in and reversing out or reversing in and driving out
- Pull up on the right-hand side of the road, reverse for about 2 car lengths, then re-join the traffic.

During the test you will drive independently for about 20 minutes by following either directions, from a SatNav or roadside direction signs, the examiner will pull you over and will explain this before you start your independent driving. The examiner will set the SatNav up for you. You cannot use your own SatNav. If you cannot see the roadside direction signs because they are missing or covered in foliage, the examiner will give you directions until you can see the next one. If you forget the instructions, you can ask the examiner for clarification, if you go off the route you will not be given a fault for taking a wrong turn. The examiner will help you get back on the route. The examiner will note down any mistakes you make during the driving test. During the Covid-19 pandemic, driving examiners will direct you back to the driving test centre if the mistake or mistakes you have made means you've already failed. The test will end early. Your driving examiner's supervisor might also sit in on your test to watch your examiner's performance. If you refuse, your test can be cancelled and you'll have to book another test and pay again, so if your instructor is also going to sit in on your test there will be four people in the car.

Type of faults that are recorded

- Dangerous Faults – these involve actual danger to the examiner, the public, property or you.
- Serious Faults – something that is potentially dangerous
- Driving Faults – this is not potentially dangerous, but if you keep making the same fault, it could become a serious fault.

REMEMBER, I like to call these mistakes, not faults.

You will fail your driving test if you make:

- More than 15 Driving faults (sometimes called minor faults)

- 1 serious or dangerous fault (sometimes called major faults)

Remember, on your practical driving test you will not be asked to do anything that you will not use in your everyday driving or in fact covered in your driving lessons. The competencies that are tested are the things you will have to do while driving alone. This is the reason the 'independent' driving section of the driving test was introduced, it was to stop learners getting a prompt from the examiner to check their mirrors and signal, as you would know as soon as the examiner gave you a direction you knew the turn was coming up, so you knew when to start your 'mirror, signal, mirror' routine.

The important thing to remember is the 'why' factor. Why do we have to drive in this way on the driving test? You should not just drive in a particular way because your instructor tells you to, or worse still, says you must do something in a certain way, just for your test. This isn't the best way to learn to be a skilled driver for life. You need to know why you should drive in a certain way, so always ask for an explanation. If your instructor cannot give you a good explanation for driving or performing a task in a certain way, other than, you must do this for your driving test, then you really need to consider changing your driving instructor or have a chat with the driving school about it.

For example, there are instructors who will say you need to check your rear-view mirror because, (here comes the 'why' factor) you need to know what is behind you. Sounds like a pantomime, doesn't it? And yes, you guessed it, it is a pantomime! This is not the real 'why' factor, and before you run to the phone to ring your instructor, this is just a standard answer some instructors give, this is not their fault, it is because this is what they were told was the 'why factor' during their training.

What is the real, 'why' factor then? The reason why you need to know what is behind you is so that you can make informed decisions while driving and choose when and where you do things. For example, if your mirror checks are good, you will spot the blue lights on an emergency vehicle in the far distance well before you hear the sirens, and therefore plan your driving accordingly. Also, when slowing down to stop you can spot drivers who are coming up behind you too fast, or they are busy changing the radio station or even worse on the phone. Seeing this potential danger simply allows you to deal with it better and reduce your risk on the road. You may even have time to change lanes, sound your horn or even stop slightly further forward. I always call the centre mirror or rear-view mirror the REPS mirror, I picked this up during my many training courses I attended in order to train fleet drivers and sales representatives, which means Rear End Protection System.

What Would You Do?

This story is about a trainer I know well.

Dave was driving on the motorway, the traffic in front was coming to a swift stop. Dave checked all his mirrors, especially his REPS mirror and identified a car behind him closing in really fast. Dave managed to change lanes at the last minute and the car behind him ploughed into the car that was in front of him before he changed lanes. The traffic had come to a standstill and the driver of the car, which would have been in front of him, got out and actually blamed Dave for the collision asking him why he had not stayed where he was so that he go hit instead...

I will leave you to draw your own conclusion as to what you would have done.

Like many city test centres, there are several examiners working in them. Some years ago, before the ADI Register was implemented, one particular Dublin lady presented herself for the test on nine occasions. She had become a cause celebre and was well known to the examiners. On the ninth test, the examiner assigned to her said that if she didn't crash her car on the test, he would pass her. She was overjoyed on passing and thanked the examiner profusely to the point of almost kissing him. Looking out the window waiting for the 2.30 pm test, the examiner observed the same lady arriving with her pupil in her fully liveried school car for the test. Talk about the blind leading the blind.

Tom Harrington – Eire

I was teaching a young teenage lad. His problem, once he got used to the car, was driving too fast, I had to keep slowing him down. I tried various techniques to stop this and he had improved. He said to me that he would not speed on his test. I replied you shouldn't speed with me.
Test day arrived and we had what I would call a near-perfect lesson. He was buzzing with confidence as we went through the gates at the old Garston test centre.
Out came the grizzled old examiner scanning the waiting room for his prey then called his name. My pupil was absolutely up for it, ready to go.

Forty minutes later they return. I walk out to the car to hear the debrief. I looked at the test sheet to see an almost clean sheet apart from the appropriate speed box which had no fewer than twelve ticks in it. The examiner said he wouldn't go above 20mph on every road. I told him that I had trouble slowing him down. When I asked him what was going on, his reply was this. "My dad told me that if I drive at 20mph everywhere I would pass my test". The examiner and I looked at each other in disbelief. The examiners parting words to the lad were, LISTEN TO YOUR INSTRUCTOR.

Colin Chown - Liverpool

Top FACT or FICTION about the driving test.

Sayings I've heard over the years about the driving test.

1. If you don't get to the maximum posted speed limit, you will fail your test.

Examiners are looking for the candidate to drive at an appropriate speed for the conditions. So, for example if it is raining, heavy traffic, children milling around or simply dangerous to drive at the speed limit the examiner will not expect or want you to drive at the maximum speed limit. However, if the conditions are good, the road is clear then the examiner will expect a test candidate to drive up to the speed limit. That's the only way they know you are safe at those speeds.

2. You are not allowed to go over 40mph as a learner driver.

Examiners may take a test candidate on a national speed limit dual carriageway road, which is certainly over 40mph. If you are helping someone, please don't restrict them to 40mph on a national speed limit road, if you don't feel confident to let them drive at 70mph when it's safe, then please just stay off these roads and let the driving instructor help them. However, this is the case in Northern Ireland, you are not allowed to travel over 45mph when learning or within the first year of driving and you must display R plates, which means Restricted Driver.

3. Drive slowly on your test so you don't have to do the full route.

The examiner will know if you are deliberately driving slowly and you will be marked down for this, meaning it might cause you to fail. I have personal experience of this. I had a pupil fail because he was going too slow on his driving test. The pupil in question was doing an extended driving test after being banned from driving, just to point out here, not everyone has to redo their driving test after a driving ban, that decision is up to the magistrates. The extended test uses the same marking system. This particular pupil wanted to show the driving examiner that they were safe, but because they didn't drive to the speed limits when conditions allowed them to, the result was a test fail, due to lack of progress, either appropriate speed or undue hesitancy.

4. You fail immediately if you speed on your driving test.

You will not fail because you went slightly over the speed limit, it is how much you went over the speed limit that matters, how long you drove over the limit and what you did to correct it. This will determine if the examiner is going to record a driving fault or not, the examiner could even record a serious fault if you are well above the speed limit or you are continually driving over the speed limit, even by a small amount, it can lead up to your test fail.

5. You will fail if you stall the car at a junction.

Stalling in the middle of a busy junction because you have moved away in the wrong gear could result in a test fail, especially if other road users have to get around you or you are blocking the junction. However, if you go to move away in the wrong gear and you immediately notice, correct the mistake and clear the junction quickly and safely, it might not even get marked as a driving fault, it is often termed a 'not worthy' fault, an expression which examiners' use when a mistake is not worthy of recording.

6. Driving examiners have a pass/fail quota.

I have covered this in a different chapter, but I'm mentioning it again as it's a comment I so often hear. As I have never been a driving examiner, I cannot really say *for absolute certainty if this is a myth or not, but let's look at the facts. There are a lot of learner drivers who try to take their test too early, this is one of the biggest reasons people fail their driving tests due to not having enough training beforehand. Also, I have sat in on countless driving tests with my own pupils. I have never witnessed a test that has resulted in a failure or in fact a pass that did not deserve the result.*

The driving test pass rate has over the years hovered around the 46% pass mark. The average between 2008 and 2020 was 46.2%, the lowest being 44.02 in 2008, the highest being 47.1 in 2013, 2014 and 2017. Apparently, for a test to be fit for purpose, there has to be about a 50% pass rate. If too many people are passing, then this could mean the test is too easy. If too many people are failing, then the test could be deemed too difficult. This was said at an MSA (Motor Schools Association) conference many years ago, in fact this was the first ever conference I attended. I remember being in awe as this was the chief driving examiner who spoke about this on stage. I have added a link to an article that was published in the Guardian Newspaper back in 2002, the link is in Appendix 9. This also applies to the test routes and the examiners themselves. There must be some sort of pass rate to make a test fit for purpose. If an examiner has a pass rate that is much higher or lower than the other examiners at the same test centre, that examiner will be assessed or checked. Now, as we all know, most people and yes examiners too, don't like being assessed so the examiners might subconsciously try to keep within their test centre pass rate.

7. You are more likely to pass at the end of the week than at the start.

This myth relates to above, because people think the examiner has to alter the test results on a Friday to fit in with the suggested quota, but surely this can work both for and against you. It's better not to think about it or book the test for a Wednesday, only joking! Just book the day best for you.

8. Examiners are just out to fail you.

This myth has been passed around by people who have failed their driving test and didn't want to take responsibility for it. They want to blame someone for the failure. Again, in my experience when sitting in on driving tests, examiners often give the benefit of the doubt, especially if the test candidate is driving well and above the standard required to pass. I am 100% sure that all the people who get first-time passes would not say the examiners are out to fail you. When people fail the driving test, they either blame the instructor or the examiner, so many people say 'the examiner failed me on...' It was not the examiner who failed you, it was you who failed your driving test, either because of a silly mistake or you were just not ready.

9. Some drive test centres are easier to pass in than others.

This could be true. Remote out of town driving test centres could be easier to pass in than test centres in busy towns and cities. Although, if you stick to your local test centre you are more likely to feel comfortable with the roads and environment that the examiner will take you on, which can give you an advantage over a remote test centre where you are not familiar with the environment. Every advanced driving test I have taken and passed has been on unfamiliar roads and routes. Again, if your driving instructor is just taking you only on test routes, you are being short-changed because it's not the roads you are driving on that matters, it's the rules you follow. You should be taught to read the road and follow the rules, so you can drive on any road and not be left to work it out for yourself after you have passed. After all most roads are grey tarmac with lines on if you know what the rules mean, the lines mean, and what the signs mean you should be okay. I'm not saying for one second we are all comfortable driving on roads we don't know, but we should have enough knowledge and skill to negotiate them safely.

Apparently in 2019

Inveraray had a pass rate of　87.5%

Compared to

Birmingham (The Pavilion) with 28.9%

A pupil was driving to the test centre on her test day. Driving down a dual carriageway with a grass verge at the side she pointed out two magpies and quoted, "Two for Joy." As we drove past one took off and flew into the back wheel of the car. I looked in the door mirror and saw it dead in the gutter. She asked what I was looking at. I told a white lie and said I didn't know, there was just something in the gutter.

Luckily, she didn't see it and went on to pass her test for the first time.

Joan Cupit – Liverpool

Many moons ago I was training to be an Ordit Instructor and was sitting in the back observing a training session. About halfway through the session the instructor and trainee decided it was time for a cigarette. As somewhere safe to pull over was being looked for, a Chrysler Voyager came alongside and cut in front of the car we were in. Before I had a chance to wonder what was happening, I heard, "Armed police get out of the car with your hands in the air." We were out immediately and had guns pointing at us. Cool and calmly the instructor wound down the window and said, "Can I help you, officer?" At which point I seem to recall someone else saying," the Wrong car!" Looking further down the road two others were standing waving with arms in the air to grab our attention. They stood directly behind a Renault Clio, which incidentally was exactly the same as the one we were in. Turned out they were on training exercises from Hutton Police HQ.

John Airey – Darwin, Lancashire

Chapter 8

Driving Examiners

Are examiners out to fail you?

There are so many stories, myths in every area regarding certain test centres or certain examiners. As you can see from the previous chapter, from mythical examiners that fail everyone, to those who have a quota to meet and have to fail so many in a day. In my local area, we had an examiner nicknamed Fail 'em Jones. The legend was that he would just fail everyone, however, I've had many of my pupils pass with Mr. Jones. It just so happened that the original Fail 'em Jones, had retired many years previously and another Mr. Jones started working in the same area, who was unfortunately saddled with the same title. I also knew of another examiner nicknamed The Smiling Assassin. He got this name simply because when he met the pupil at the beginning of the test he always smiled. But of course, not all of those pupils who took their test with him, passed. When a pupil failed with him, the instructor said it was because he was The Smiling Assassin. I have sat in on tests many times over the years, and I know many examiners. I am yet to find a Fail 'em Jones, or one with a quota to fill.

I sat in the back of a car on a test, the learner driver was on a dual carriageway and got behind a funeral procession. The examiner asked, "Do you know the deceased?" The learner on the test said no, then thankfully took the hint and overtook the procession.

I sat in on another test with a very tall pupil of mine, who I had previously told during lessons that if another driver shows courtesy, you can raise your hand and thank them. It was a warm day on the test, and the windows were down. During the test another driver had shown courtesy to us, but rather than merely raising his hand in thanks, he put his long arm fully out of the window and gave a big old wave. Thankfully we were stationary in traffic at the time, so while highly unusual it wasn't a problem. My pupil did a few funny things like this throughout the test, but he drove very well. In the end, when the examiner told him he had passed, he replied saying. "Have I passed, have I passed?" the examiner added,
"Well put it this way, I'm not going to go through that again."

Another memory I have about the same examiner. I'm in the back of the car on a test. We got back to the test centre car park. The examiner then asked, "Can you please drive forward into one of these bays on the left, don't worry about reversing this is not part of the test just drive forward into the bay." So, the learner got themselves smack bang in the middle of two bays, two wheels in one bay and two wheels in the other, the examiner turned and said,
"Yes, perhaps these two bays will do."

What training do examiners have?

Driving examiners come from all walks of life, including some who have been driving instructors themselves. Believe it or not, it is not a natural progression for driving instructors to become examiners. To become a driving examiner, you undergo an intensive four-week training course to which your own driving is tested to a very high standard, and you will have to perform these manoeuvres:

- Reverse parking.
- Pulling up on the right, reversing two car lengths then re-joining the traffic.
- Driving into a parking bay then reversing out.
- Reversing into a parking bay then driving out.

The examiners' test used to include reverse around the corner and a turn in the road, but they are no longer done as their test needs to mirror the L-Test. At the end of each week, there is an exam, either in driving, on knowledge, or procedures. They have to pass all of these exams every week just to stay on the course. Once they pass the full course and start their job as an examiner they are closely monitored; their pass rate is also monitored to ensure that all tests are conducted fairly. Now, this is where the fun begins; if the new examiner has a too high or too low pass rate, they will have to go for further training.

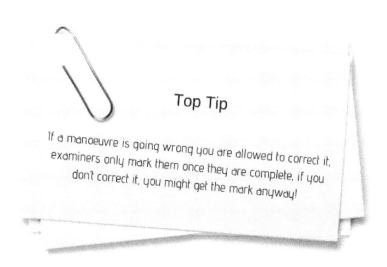

Top Tip

If a manoeuvre is going wrong you are allowed to correct it, examiners only mark them once they are complete, if you don't correct it, you might get the mark anyway!

Maybe, as I have mentioned in the facts and fiction in the driving test section, this is where people think there are quotas. It's a big misconception that examiners have to fail so many pupils. Realistically, it is easy to see why people might think this is the case, but there are so many people who are learning to drive and going in for their test too early, when they are simply not prepared for the driving test, let alone for driving solo in the real world. Some people go for a driving test, just so they can give it a go, to see if they pass, which may also risk their or their instructor's car and possibly the instructor's livelihood. This is just a waste of money and can seriously knock your confidence, as detailed in a previous chapter about instructor misconceptions. Apparently, there are some instructors who actually encourage their pupils to put in for a test too early, in order to destroy a learner's confidence, thus resulting in the need to buy even more driving lessons, which they might have not needed if their confidence had not been damaged. Bearing this in mind, it is apparent that neither examiners nor test centres have to fill a quota, as it's almost done for them anyway by people taking their test too early.

The thing to remember is that the driving examiners are human, they are drivers themselves, and believe it or not they have feelings too. Passing someone is a tremendous responsibility. The last thing an examiner would want to do is put a driver on the road before they are ready to tackle driving solo and keep themselves and other road users safe. Imagine how an examiner would feel if they passed a pupil, and they found out that a week later the pupil they had passed killed themselves or someone else on the road. This is from a retired driving examiner.

"As an ex driving examiner of 23 years, hopefully I can help you also with the myths attached to the driving test. There are three legal requirements which must be carried out:

1) Reverse exercise.
2) Angle start.
3) Minimum of two normal stops.

It is important you are with an instructor who has fully prepared you to handle any situation (risk management). Anything you're not sure of whilst on the test, your examiner will clarify it for you. I wish you every success and safe driving for the future."

E Jones - P.S. I'm not Fail 'em Jones!

Examiners are human too!

A student returned after five minutes of their test to inform the waiting room that his test was terminated, as the examiner had filled his pants after a curry the night before. Still laughing now three years on.

Dave Robinson, Birkenhead

Having been to the test centre several times with this particular learner - it was a surprise to me when this happened.

"I would like you to turn right at the roundabout - 2nd exit," I said.

The learner replied, "Turn right at the roundabout?"

So, I clarified, "Yes that is correct, turn right at the roundabout 2nd exit. They replied again,

"RIGHT? At the roundabout?"

"Yes, that is correct" Sussing something may not be well I pinched myself. For a third time, the learner said,

"Right, at the roundabout?"

"Yes please," I replied.

"Well, you have no idea how difficult it is to turn right anti-clockwise against the flow of traffic at a normal speed approach"

Fortunately, I was able to intervene with the dual controls. Ah well, the life of an instructor.

David Thomson – Wishaw, Scotland

Chapter 9

Now You Have Passed, What Next?

Emily Higgins Huyton
Pass Certificate

Is passing your driving test the end of the journey?

Passing a practical driving test can be one of the most memorable moments for anyone, ask around if you don't believe me, everyone you ask will easily remember their own story of passing their driving test. You only have to tell someone you are taking your test and they will tell you in great detail what happened on their test, either the one they passed or the one(s) they failed. While networking or out socially, I told people I was a driving instructor. I got these stories all the time, so I told people I worked in a supermarket, then I didn't have to listen to yet another driving test story while they were using their very selective memory! Eventually, I came clean at networking events as I was there for my driving school business looking for work for my team of instructors.

Traditionally, it was always the driving instructor who drove you home after your driving test whether you passed or failed. The reason given for this is it was deemed unsafe for you to drive whilst either feeling very upset that you failed or thrilled that you have passed. It would allow you to use your phone on the way home to inform people of your result. I feel that it is an opportunity lost if you don't drive home after your test pass or fail. At some point in your life, you will have to drive with a heightened emotion whatever that might be, it could be anger, joy, stress, grief or excitement, who knows what life brings us. So, why not experience this the first time in a relatively safe environment with your instructor sitting next to you, who can and will take action should things go wrong? You will at least be able to know how it feels driving in an emotional state.

After all the congratulations die down, reality hits. No longer will an instructor be there to bounce ideas around with you, help you try new things or offer support, you are on your own. For many this is a heady experience, for others this is terrifying. Statistics suggest that some newly passed drivers don't feel comfortable driving on their own after passing their driving test. If this were true, we have to ask if they had been taught to just pass their test? If so, it's little wonder that they don't feel comfortable driving on their own after passing their driving test.

After you pass your test, it is easy to think it is all over, however; it is just the beginning. There are lots of post-test training which can be more relaxing as there is no test to pass unless of course, you want to do an advanced driving test.

Often, a new driver's confidence grows faster than their skill, which can take a nosedive, as they allow all the habits they have witnessed over the years creep into their driving.

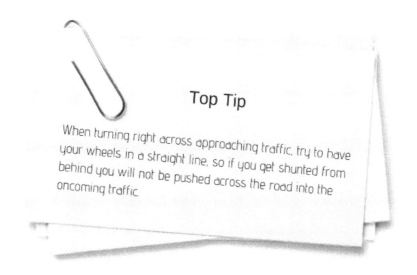

Top Tip

When turning right across approaching traffic, try to have your wheels in a straight line, so if you get shunted from behind you will not be pushed across the road into the oncoming traffic.

There is a lot to be said for holding on to the skill you have developed with your driving instructor and the skill you used to pass your driving test. Please hold on to that skill whilst you are gaining experience on the road, this will keep you one step ahead of most of the people you are sharing the road with. New drivers are blamed for being in or causing collisions on the road. Whilst the proportion of new drivers being involved in collisions is very high compared to other age groups, and you are more likely to have a collision within the first six months of driving or within the first 1000 miles. It does not follow that experienced drivers who have let their skill level decline whilst getting into lazy or bad habits will not be involved in a collision. So, instead of having skill or experience, why not have both?

A question often asked is, should you display the green P plates, at the moment there is no legislation to say you have to display them? There are two schools of thoughts on this. One is that most drivers will give you more room on the road and forgive you for making mistakes if they can see you are displaying a P plate, however, the other school of thought is that some drivers may bully you knowing that you are a new driver.

Having driven for so many years, often with L plates on my car, I can tell the difference in how other motorists treat you on the road, even when I was driving alone to my next leaner, I would encounter more bad manners on the road while displaying the L plates on then when I was not displaying them. My personal opinion on P plates is that if you feel you really need to display them and cannot do without them, then maybe you're not as confident in your own driving as you should be. It will be far better to take a bit of post-test training and build your confidence. As I've said, this is my opinion, if displaying P plates makes you feel better, please display them, but do not use them as an excuse for your own failings as a driver.

Many proactive drivers will consider further training such as the Pass Plus course, which is a post-test course of at least six hours, covering:

- Town and city centre driving
- Dual carriageways
- All-weather driving
- Night driving
- Country or rural roads
- Motorways

Pass Plus is currently dying a death, perhaps by the time you read this, it may not be a recognised course at all. This is because a good driving instructor will have taught you dual carriageways, rural or country roads, town and city driving and hopefully night driving, but of course it depends on the time of day or year you do your driving lessons. It's difficult to incorporate night driving during the summer months or driving in all weather conditions and even the most professional of driving instructors can't make it snow.

Another thing some instructors cannot cover while you are learning to drive, is motorway driving. This may be because of the distance a motorway is from where you are learning to drive. For example, if you live in south Cornwall, Scotland or Mid Wales motorways might just be too far away for a pupil to drive to during a lesson. Many instructors in the past used the Pass Plus as a way of doing motorway lessons, but learners can now drive on a motorway as part of their training. By law they must be with a fully qualified driving instructor in a dual-controlled car. Please don't get Auntie Joan to take you on the motorway as part of your private practice, both of you will break the law, and your insurance will be void.

I had the pleasure of taking my daughter Emily on the motorway to visit my Mum and Dad in Ulverston, Cumbria while she was learning; she drove on the M57, M58, M6, and the M62 all in one day. I have to say it was a bit nerve-racking in the first five minutes on the busy M6, but after that it was easy. We also went into a service area so she could get practice doing this too. You might already know that motorways are the safest roads we can drive on, and once you are on one it is just about driving in a straight line and learning how to change lanes safely and keeping space around your car. The most challenging bits are joining and leaving the motorway. When you practice, try to get on and off as much as you can. All of which you will also cover on national speed limit dual carriageways which can be more challenging than motorways.

Where do collisions happen?

Where we live, play and work.

- Urban areas 63%
- Rural & open roads 33%
- Motorways 5%

I think I might have been the first parent who took their child on the motorway with a provisional licence. I have no way of knowing this though, as some instructors were out at one-minute past midnight on June 4th, 2018. Just so, they could claim to be the first instructor to take a learner on a motorway. The things people do for a bit of publicity, a bit like writing a book…

Some people say that the Pass Plus has apparently been ruined by our very own industry with narrow minded driving instructors apparently taking backhanders and simply signing all the Pass Plus paperwork. Some were signing the pupil off declaring that they have done the six hours training and stating that they had reached the Pass Plus standard, when all they have done is sign the form and have not actually taken the pupil out on the road at all.

Perhaps insurance companies were not seeing any evidence that doing the extra driver training was reducing the number of collisions that new drivers who had completed the Pass Plus were having. We can only speculate that if these new drivers had been given the proper training, the figures could have shown a different picture. It was believed that the extra training the Pass Plus would give drivers should have resulted in fewer collisions.

If you don't see the benefit from doing any further training, then why would you do it? When I say this, I mean financial benefit as this is all some new drivers wanted, cheaper insurance, they did not actually want the extra training. The day we pass our driving test we are usually on an emotional high and we think, that's it. This is when we are most at risk, and unfortunately for some drivers it will take several near misses, a collision or even a death on the road to realise that it is vital to keep improving our driving skills by continued training or development and by using self-identification of mistakes, self-analysis and self-remedial action. This is what client centred learning or teaching is all about, giving our learners the skills to self-reflect and take responsibility for all their own actions and failings and do something about it.

If the Pass Plus is to improve driving skills as intended, then maybe there is room or a replacement Pass Plus test? A test where there is evidence that training had taken place. Pass Plus has to be taken within the first two years of driving, if you were going to get a reduction in insurance premiums. Many insurance companies no longer recognise this course as much as they used to, because the only evidence they had to go on was that the collision figures for new drivers did not seem to reduce even after the Pass Plus course.

Driver Development

What can you do if you don't want to take another driving test? Simply take some Driver Development sessions or a Driving Assessment with your local approved driving instructor. It is best to choose an instructor who has advanced driving qualifications, because if you choose an instructor whose specialty is teaching learner drivers, you may end up having a driving lesson targeted at entry level. This is the last thing you want and it may be counterproductive.

Any trainer worth their salt will know that even a bit of over instruction can lead to underperformance of the trainee and can destroy any confidence they may have. It can also create resentment of the instructor.

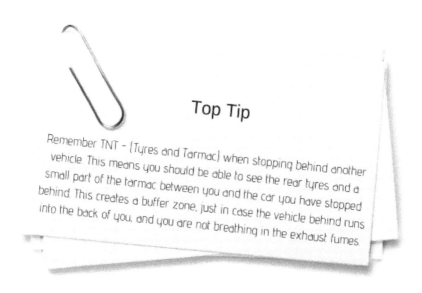

Top Tip

Remember TNT – (Tyres and Tarmac) when stopping behind another vehicle. This means you should be able to see the rear tyres and a small part of the tarmac between you and the car you have stopped behind. This creates a buffer zone, just in case the vehicle behind runs into the back of you, and you are not breathing in the exhaust fumes.

You may also, depending on your job, have a driver assessment and/or training. Many companies are now embracing the safety of their employees who drive for work. Unfortunately, this is sometimes done as a box ticking exercise, but when done properly it can be very rewarding both for the driver and the company. Some insurance companies also offer a discount for having all the drivers regularly assessed or have their knowledge updated regularly. Companies can facilitate classroom sessions for their drivers, which can be very cost effective. I feel that the best way of helping drivers and keeping them safe while at work is to use behavioural change techniques or explore the human aspects of driving. In my experience working with full licence holders there is little point in trying to change their driving habits while you are in the car with them, they must want to change and have good reason for doing so. Full licence holders will do what you ask them to do on a training course, but as soon as they are out on their own again with nobody watching them, they will revert to old habits. We must give them strategies for change; however, it is best that we do bolt-on some education and refresh our knowledge of the rules and regulations for the roads today. Most drivers I have worked with do not want to be on a course, but really enjoy the experience. You can, of course, do all this in the car. Any driver training a company undertakes, should be bespoke to them and tailored to suit their individual needs as a company and for their drivers.

Key point to remember is the new drivers act, which states your license will be revoked if you collect six penalty points or more within the first two years of driving. This means you will have to do the following…

- Apply and pay for a new provisional driving licence.
- Apply, pay for and pass your theory test.
- Apply, pay for and pass your practical driving test.

To avoid having to do any of this simply drive as you have been driving with your driving instructor and as you drove on your driving test when you passed.

A fixed penalty speeding offence will carry three points, being caught holding a handheld communication device, will get you six points. If you have to go to court for a more serious offence, you could look at anything from points, a fine or even a ban. You will find loads more information about using mobile phones while driving in chapter 10.

Advanced driver training is easy to access. There is a test at the end of the training, but you do not have to take the test if you don't want to, you can simply benefit from the extra driver training. I have known some drivers who do not get to the standard to pass the advanced test but are still commended for improving their driving.

This extra training is done in your own time, at a pace that suits you, and in your own car. If you take the test it can lead onto cheaper insurance, however, this is not a guarantee.

There are several different advanced tests now available and depending on who you talk to will depend on which one you choose. Each organisation will say theirs is the best or the highest standard, I just think any extra training is going to be worth it, in more ways than one. Don't let the word 'advanced' put you off, it's just more driving, better driving, thinking driving. Thinking driving was a term used for drivers who thought about driving when they are driving (imagine that!) instead of just going into autopilot or putting the world to rights either in our heads or having deep and meaningful conversations with passengers.

Remember the airbag deployment area when steering, if you have your arms over the wheel when it goes off, you could end up breaking your wrist with your own face!

The advanced driving tests.

The DVSA L-test is just an entry level test, although in order to pass the L-test today you have to have a greater level of skill and knowledge than I had, when I passed my L-test. I know everyone would benefit from doing some advanced driver training, perhaps it should be a mandatory requirement of keeping your licence? I'm not suggesting a re-test that could result in you losing your licence, instead perhaps some form of refresher training. In fact, many people who have attended speed awareness courses say that everyone should do a refresher course like this. They always say this after they have completed the course, strangely enough they don't say it before the start of their course. As the saying goes, 'you don't know what you don't know.'

In no particular order, the advanced tests are...

The IAM RoadSmart (Institute of Advanced Motorists)

This was the first advanced test I tackled. Remember, I took it in a transit van, yes, a white one. I have also recently re-taken my IAM test to celebrate 25 years as an advanced driver. I gained the IAM First. Yes, the girl still has it! I have to say a big thank you to the St. Helens and District Group of Advanced Motorists who had to put up with me.

Anyway, this test is a pass or fail test based on the standard of the overall drive. It lasts for about one hour and covers all types of roads. You can make some mistakes on this test, but they must not be consistent or break any traffic laws, there will also be an element of reversing. In order to gain the IAM First, you have to give a commentary drive or use 'spoken thoughts' during part of the test. The training is done over several hours with the observed sessions one to two weeks apart. You will be invited to take the test once the observer feels you are ready to pass it, hence the test has a great pass rate, as people only tend to put in for the test when they are actually ready and have had enough training. The test is usually conducted by either a serving or retired traffic police, however, there are a few advanced examiners who are chosen from civilian drivers because their driving and dedication is at the same standard. These are usually drivers who drive or ride several different vehicles, such as motorcycles, heavy goods, and buses.

Once you pass the IAM test, it's with you for life, as long as you keep paying your membership. If you want to keep your standard up, it is best to be reassessed regularly. The IAM now has a fellowship, whereas you are assessed every three years as a Fellow of the IAM.

The IAM Special Assessment

The IAM Special Assessment was another available test, but I don't think these are now being offered. This was 1.5 hours long and a high level of driving is required. You will also be asked to give a commentary drive of a greater length than the normal IAM test. Again, once passed that's it for life.

The IAM also offers the advanced riding test, young driver assessments, mature driver reviews, members assessments, fellowship assessments and much more. Then there is the IAM RoadSmart Master's programme which helps drivers take their talent to the next level. Building on the individual's skills as an existing advanced road user. Links to the IAM Roadsmart and the St. Helen's Group are in Appendix 9.

"The IAM RoadSmart Advanced Driving Course is a fantastic way of boosting confidence and improving driving skill. The course is divided into sessions and each session lasts a couple of hours. Focus is on specific skills developing a wide range of advanced driving competencies such as, control, observation, timing, optimum road positioning, ability to deal with unpredictable roads and other road users' behaviour. These skills make better drivers and riders and ultimately reduce road risk. In the 60 years since IAM was founded, half a million people have qualified as advanced drivers and demonstrated their higher level of skill. All of which obtained on our flagship Advanced Driver course, which is Quality Assured by the DVSA.

As well as gaining recognition for driving skill, once qualified full IAM member status is obtained and desirable insurance rates are a benefit worth having. New members tell us they feel more confident and safer on the road after our courses and having an Advanced Driver qualification can add brownie points to a CV." - IAM Roadsmart.

The RoADAR Advanced Test
RoSPA's Advanced Driving and Riding.

RoADAR is an arm of RoSPA, The Royal Society for the Prevention of Accidents, it is now normally just referred to as RoSPA Advanced Drivers and Riders. As with the IAM training, the RoSPA training is usually done on a Sunday morning when local groups meet up. The test is very similar to the IAM test, it lasts for about one hour and covers all types of roads. Again, you can make some mistakes, but they must not be consistent or break any traffic laws, there will also be an element of reversing and a commentary drive. The major difference between the IAM and the RoSPA is that RoSPA is a graded test. You can still either pass or fail. However, when you pass the RoSPA you are awarded a Bronze, Silver or Gold grade. As mentioned in the above paragraph the IAM also has a grading system now, either a pass or an IAM First.

Obviously, the Gold is the grade everyone wants to get, this creates a competitive edge either between you and the other people taking the test, the other members, or when you compete against yourself so want to retake the test to get a better grade.

Another difference between IAM and RoSPA is that with the RoSPA you will automatically be invited to a re-test every three years for free.

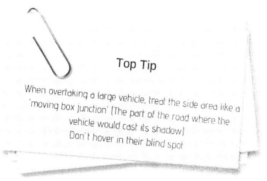

Top Tip

When overtaking a large vehicle, treat the side area like a 'moving box junction' (The part of the road where the vehicle would cast its shadow) Don't hover in their blind spot

Both RoSPA and IAM training is usually conducted by willing volunteers or observers, who have taken the test and passed with a good grade, and of course have a passion for road safety, unlike Approved Driving Instructors, DBS checks are not required for Observers. They have a national policy. Groups and Observers operate under a code of conduct. The main requirement for an Observer is to pass a set of competencies that meet the Institute of the Motor Industry (IMI) requirements. Fully approved driving instructors are checked at least every four years by the DBS (Disclosure & Barring Service, this was previously called a CRB check). There are a few driving instructors who give up their time voluntarily to work with their local advanced driving groups. If you are not sure what checks have been made, ask them. If they are an approved driving instructor, they will be happy to show you their instructors' licence, which is usually displayed in the windscreen of their car.

If they are an approved instructor and they refuse to show you, this might be because they are volunteering and not being paid, so they don't need to display it. However, approved driving instructors have worked really hard to gain their ADI licence, so it is likely they will be more than happy to show it to you.

The Diamond Advanced

If you want to be trained in advanced driving by a professional driving instructor or weekends and mornings are not convenient for you, maybe your ROSPA or IAM trainers can't accommodate your availability, this might be the test for you, or like me, just do all of them.

The Diamond Advanced test is based on the DVSA marking system; therefore, it is a fault-based test, but at a much higher standard than the L test. It is marked the same way as the DVSA test, which means you will be marked for driving faults, you are only allowed six driving faults, or minor faults. If you make one dangerous or serious fault, it will just result in a failure, like the L-test (remember we like to call these mistakes not faults.) It is a one-hour test and two of the manoeuvres will be tested. This is any two including, turn in the road, reversing left around a corner, reversing right around a corner and a reverse parking exercise, either on a road, (parallel parking) or into a parking bay.

Once you pass this test, that's it for life, no membership is required.

The Diamond Special Test, now called The Diamond Elite Test.

This is a step up from the Diamond Test. This lasts at least 90 minutes, again based on the DVSA marking system, therefore fault based. Your driving must be of a very high standard for you to pass this test, you are only allowed two driving faults and you are not allowed to make the same fault twice, for example you are not allowed to miss two mirror checks. You are not allowed any serious or dangerous faults.

In this 90-minute test, you will be asked to do at least two of the manoeuvres, this could be any or all of the following, turn in the road, reversing left around a corner, reversing right around a corner and a reverse parking exercise, either on a road, (parallel parking) or into a parking bay. You will also be asked to perform a commentary drive for at least 10 minutes during the drive. If you pass the Diamond Elite test, you can then train to become a Diamond Advanced Examiner. All the diamond advanced tests are conducted by fully qualified Approved Driving Instructors.

RAC – Royal Automobile Club Advanced Test

As far as I am aware this test is no longer available. It was designed for any motorist to take, and you were graded silver gold or platinum. I gained the platinum standard. The test was conducted by BSM (British School of Motoring) approved driving instructors, it was an hour-long test taken in your local area and was based on the DVSA marking system.

The Cardington Special Test, now called the DVSA special test.

This driving test is only available to approved driving instructors, Cardington assessed compulsory basic training (CBT) instructors, direct access scheme trainers and DVSA enhanced rider scheme trainers. It is probably one of the most expensive tests to take as you have to take it in Cardington which is in Bedfordshire. Great, if you live in Bedfordshire, but not so much if you have to travel there and factor in an overnight stay. It lasts for an hour and thirty minutes and a high level of skill is required to pass this test. It is graded A to D, and you also get an overall grading of fail, bronze, silver and gold. Unfortunately, I only got a B grade. I never got to take it again, so far, because of the expense involved.

Chapter 10

Driver Behaviour

Do you ever reflect on your own driver behaviour?

Imagine you have already passed your driving test, and you are driving alone. Are you really going to keep doing what you have been doing on your driving lessons and test?

In short, probably not. Once you are driving on your own you enter the expressive phase of driving. This essentially means that we start to express our personality in our driving. You drive in a way you feel is socially acceptable, or the social norm, so if you have witnessed other drivers in your family or friendship circle driving in a particular way you will see this as the way to drive, maybe not the way your instructor has helped you develop.

This expressive stage cannot be seen by anyone else because, as soon as someone else is in the car with you, they become an influence on your driving. No matter who they are, we always want to impress our passengers in whatever way we think they might be impressed. Driving fast to impress friends is an example of this. Even worse, sometimes people who drive too fast think the people in the car are impressed even when they are obviously scared and asking the driver to slow down.

Remember, we are all responsible for our ABC of driving - Attitude, Behaviour and Choice, you are only responsible for your ABC of driving and you cannot change anyone else's.

Excellent instructors will try to make your driving lessons resemble real driving as much as possible. For example, they will help you learn things which are NOT on the driving test, or on your particular test routes.

Even as I write this book, I have a learner driver who, despite having taken two practical driving tests with another instructor and having spent the best part of £1000 for the pleasure, has never driven over 40mph or used the fifth gear! The reason for this is because the learner's previous instructor, despite the pupil living ten minutes away from a driving test centre, had chosen a test centre which was much further away that it was local to the instructor and they knew the test routes. Incidentally, most of the routes this instructor knew wouldn't require the learner going over 40mph on their test.

Imagine having to learn how to get to 70mph on a busy dual carriageway for the first time on your own.

Some things good driving instructors will teach you, as part of your normal driving lessons are driving with friends, and yes sometimes they actually invite your friends to come with you on a driving lesson. Driving with music of your choice at the volume you would have it at, opening windows and changing the temperature controls on the move. Some of these actions have all now been brought into the new modern driving test. It might not be long before we have to eat a sandwich on the driving test (you know I am only joking, right?).

Top Tip

It is the small things we do or don't do on the road that make all the difference, not the big things.

We were talking about attitude, so let's explore where it all comes from. When do we start to develop a driving attitude?

Many of our behaviours are learnt from other people, especially the people who have driven us around as children. Some behaviour comes from the culture we are brought up in, hence the saying, 'everyone does it.'

As discussed in a previous chapter, many people learn to drive as children from the age of two or three. They sit there in the car while they are being driven around and absorb what they see as acceptable behaviour behind the wheel.

This has an enormous impact on driving attitude for life, because you can imagine what can happen to a young person the minute they have passed their driving test and they are driving the car with nobody watching them. Many will 'revert to type' (which is to return to usual behaviour or form after a temporary change) and copy the behaviour they have witnessed their parents getting away with.

The sad thing is, this driving attitude may cause the driver to get it wrong, sometimes with fatal consequences.

Unfortunately, there are driving instructors who display terrible driving to their learners and family, and sadly have a poor attitude to road safety, their industry and other instructors. You would think driving instructors being 'fit and proper' people would show a bit of empathy to each other, for the small minority who enter our industry this is sadly not the case.

This brings us to the debate on skill versus experience. Many experienced drivers will blame new or young drivers as causing all the problems on the road. Once you have completed a great driver training course and passed your driving test; you will have a high level of skill. But, if you have simply had just enough training in order to pass your test or if you have rushed through an intensive course, you could be more at risk. This comes down to retention, taking time to train properly and develop skills until they become second nature will lessen the risk. Once you have the skill, you will need to keep perfecting and improving it rather than letting it slip in order to try to fit in with everyone else.

Experience can fool you especially if it's the wrong sort of experience. Every time we have a near miss or drive above the legal speed limit and get away with it we simply build up our 'what's worked' bias.

When I have been training with full licence holders who have been driving for some time, they frequently say they have so many bad habits. If this was true, why would they want to keep the bad habits? If driving was a sport or hobby, they would not want to keep doing it badly, they would want to improve, wouldn't they? It takes effort to change these behaviours, and people don't like making the effort, especially if they can't see any benefits. It is far easier to just simply keep on doing what they have always done.

I can't stress this enough that there used to be a sense of pride in driving well and being courteous on the road. This appears to have been lost, apart from the small percentage of the driving population who carry to complete an advanced driving test. If only insurance companies based their premiums on good driving and give discounts to those drivers who undergo regular driver training. I know we have no claims discounts, but I feel this does not go far enough. Drivers who continually improve and can evidence this by taking an advanced driving test every few years should be rewarded.

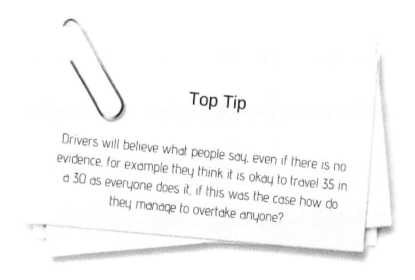

Top Tip

Drivers will believe what people say, even if there is no evidence, for example they think it is okay to travel 35 in a 30 as everyone does it, if this was the case how do they manage to overtake anyone?

I will not say it is easy to change; it isn't, but it is something anyone can do with some effort and persistence. You just need to want to change and give yourself permission to do so. The first thing to do is to recognise you need to change or make some minor changes in your own attitude and behaviour behind the wheel. Once you do this and identify the areas you need to change, the rest can come easily.

Consider re-reading the chapter regarding 'Advanced Driving', think about how many people are being killed and injured on our roads every day, consider how you would feel if you hurt or even kill someone on the road. What effect would you have on them, their families and your family? Whatever works for you, then work on the skill, keep perfecting those skills and get or keep the pride you have in driving well.

Using your mobile phone while driving

Using mobile phones while driving seems to be the modern driving epidemic. I'm sure I'm not the only person who sees other drivers using a mobile phone while driving. It always surprises me when I see someone on their phone while driving a modern, possibly expensive vehicle which is likely to be fitted with Bluetooth technology, and the driver still has their mobile phone in their hand while driving. They think it is perfectly safe to drive while talking on the phone.

The two main comparisons I hear are, if you are allowed to talk to the passenger why can't you talk on your phone? The other one is that people say that they are experienced enough at driving to keep their eyes on the road and use their mobile phone simultaneously.

There are very clear and real explanations why you can't use your mobile phone while driving, but these reasons are not always considered.

People say it is more distracting to talk to a passenger than it is to talk on a mobile phone, this is not true. It is more distracting to use your phone than talking to the passenger sitting next to you. It's called cognitive distraction. The cognitive (the need to think) demand of a phone conversation requires much more of our cognitive brain function to have a conversation on the phone than it does in person. I understand why this might be a bit confusing, after all it's just talking isn't it? Well, no, talking on the phone causes the driver much more distraction than talking to a passenger. We also have a lot of our communication values, research shows that about 55% of our communication is non-verbal, gestures, facial expressions and even skin colour change. None of this is there for us when we are having a remote conversation, meaning we need to concentrate more on the conversation when it is remote, our minds are busy building pictures of the conversation. We 'think' in images not in words, so when someone is talking about something, we are picturing them in our minds. To illustrate this, I am going to ask you a question. What colour is your front door? Did you picture it? I bet you did, and you didn't think of the word blue either. If you have a blue front door that is, you just pictured your blue front door. Also, our passengers, whether or not we like it, are a second pair of eyes on the road and they are often helping the driver. Ask yourself how many times you have helped a driver while being a passenger, by saying watch out for those traffic lights, or watch out for that cyclist? They help us, whether or not we want them to, and this includes passengers who don't even drive.

Some people claim they can multitask, while you are at home this may be true, but never while in the car. What scientific research has found is that multitasking does not exist. We simply cannot do two cognitive tasks at once. For example, the act of the telephone conversation is cognitive, and the act of driving is cognitive too, the human brain can only do one at a time. Think about it, can you watch a film and closely follow it while talking to someone on the phone? The answer is no, every time.

We just won't admit it. But driving is very different. While driving there is an ever-changing dynamic safety critical environment and having a conversation on the phone at the same time means your brain has to flip between tasks. If something happens, and your brain needs to flip from the phone conversation mode to the driving mode, a second's delay can mean the difference between life or death.

The law had to be changed regarding mobile phones, to make it easier for people to understand the law. You have always had to have full control of your vehicle at all times. Realistically, you could have been prosecuted for not having full control of your vehicle while using your hand-held mobile phone, in fact doing anything that takes away your control of the vehicle can come under careless driving. You could say that careless driving is doing anything that you would not do on a driving test, or not doing something that you would do, after all you wouldn't eat a sandwich while on your driving test.

If there is a road traffic accident resulting in death and you were on the phone, you could end up being prosecuted with death by dangerous driving which carries up to a 14-year prison sentence, which in the future may be extended to life in prison. On the other end of the scale if you just get caught using a hand-held mobile phone when driving you will get six points and a £200 on the spot fixed penalty. There used to be an option to do a police diversionary course, but most police services don't even give you this option now. The likely reason for this is that they feel you have opted to use your phone while you are driving, you cannot accidentally take or make a phone call while driving. There is now a push to ban hands-free in cars too.

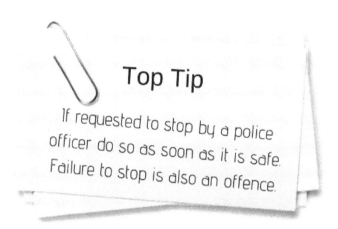

Top Tip

If requested to stop by a police officer do so as soon as it is safe. Failure to stop is also an offence.

There are two schools of thought on this. It's convenient to phone home while you are stuck in traffic to let your family know that you will be late, and you could say it is convenient to make or receive calls from your customers, but you are not giving your customer your 100% attention either. One lady, for example, has been prosecuted for causing death by dangerous driving because she killed somebody in a road traffic collision, and it was proved that she was on a conference call for 40 minutes prior to the collision occurring. Using hands-free is just as distracting as using a handheld phone, as it is the conversation that is the distraction. If you are spotted making a hands-free call and your driving drops below what can be reasonably expected from a driver, you can be pulled up and prosecuted too, again, this would come under careless driving.

Seriously, and I know I have mentioned this in a previous chapter, but it is so important, and I will say it all again, if you are a new driver who has been driving for less than two years and is caught holding a phone, it's game over. In fact, if you get six points or more for any reason in your first two years, your licence will be revoked. You will have to apply and pay for a new provisional driving licence and take and pass both the theory and practical tests again.

In 2019, 11,125 drivers lost their licences under the new drivers act, that's about 31 new drivers lost their privilege to drive, every day after reaching six penalty points within two years of passing their driving test.

According to data obtained by Autotrader, 5,503 (49%) of people had insurance-related offences, with an average of;

- ❖ 14 new drivers per day caught without insurance
- ❖ 2,871 got points for speeding
- ❖ 602 were 'distracted' including using a mobile
- ❖ 115 drivers failed to stop after a collision
- ❖ 96 for alcohol-related driving
- ❖ 40 for drug offences

The reason using a mobile phone when driving is taken so seriously and the punitive aspect so great is because making a call when driving is considered a conscious choice. There are lots of rules you can accidentally break but making or receiving a phone call is not one of them. It is almost a known fact that most people when they are lost, trying to read road signs, or when they are parking in a tight spot, turn the radio down or off. So, if the radio, which is background noise, is so distracting we sometimes need to turn it off to help us concentrate, how distracting can a two-way conversation actually be?

Attitude and behaviour of your driving instructor

I have added this section because people who are paying a professional to help them or their loved one to drive should know what their driving instructor should aspire too.

I am sure you agree that we often see driving school cars being driven by the instructors so badly you may have to look twice. If people see a so-called professional driver, (a driver who imparts his/her information on to new drivers, and charges them for it,) speeding, talking on a handheld mobile phone, parking illegally, displaying hand signals which are not in the highway code and driving discourteously, then it must be acceptable behaviour for everyone, mustn't it?

If driving instructors do it, then the learner driver will simply carry on separating the 'test' from real world driving, and people will continue to be injured and killed on our roads. What chance have we got in getting our profession recognised as a profession if we cannot control our own driving behaviour and attitude on the road?

We are all road safety professionals and should never be off duty. I was going to a meeting and car sharing with another instructor, the instructor who was driving was too close to the car in front and speeding. I commented on his driving, and when I did, he told me he was off duty. I am not saying I never make a mistake; I do, but I strive not to. If I do make a mistake, I will identify it for myself, analyse it and try to stop it happening again. These are our basic core skills, and the core of all good driving instruction, helping a learner self-analyse, self-identify mistakes and rectify our faults or mistakes.

Here is a statement we should remind ourselves of, every time we drive, because if we let our standards slip then our pupils' standards will slip too.

"Today, as all days, I will drive this car according to the MSM or IPSGA routine (Information, Position, Speed, Gear, Acceleration) which is a way of approaching and negotiating hazards that is methodical, safe and leaves nothing to chance. To do this will require me to apply concentration and alertness to drive this car safely, smoothly, progressively and well. I will formulate my driving plan on what I see, what I cannot see and the circumstances I may reasonably

expect to develop. By driving my car to the MSM or IPSGA routine I will at all times observe, plan and anticipate ensuring maximum vehicle stability in response to all road and traffic conditions." Adapted from Roadcraft, the police driving manual, I have included a link in Appendix 9, there is also a link where you can take the Roadcraft quiz.

Chapter 11

Looking after your car

Did you know learners have to know which 'under the bonnet' checks should be done?

Looking after your car is vital and could save a life. If you get into this habit weekly or even daily for some checks, whether you are a high mileage driver or not you will know if something is not quite right. For example, if you are checking the oil level regularly and one week the level has gone down dramatically, then it could mean that something else is wrong or worse still you notice there is no oil on the dipstick, it allows you to get help and get it fixed while you wait at home, with the TV or the radio on and a nice hot drink. A colleague of mine recently took his car for a service at a garage, where they told him that he was lucky to get there at all, as there was no oil in the engine. Luckily, for my colleague the car was already at the garage when he found out, had he been on the motorway when the car ran out of oil and the engine seized, he would have been in serious trouble.

Many modern cars have warning systems to tell the driver when engine fluids need topping up, but I would still physically check, especially since one of our trainers told me what happened when she went to do some fleet training with a client. She told the client that she had to check all fluid levels under the bonnet before they started the fleet training. The client replied it was unnecessary to check as the car alerts him if any of the fluid levels dip. Luckily our trainer informed the client that she still had to stick to protocol and physically check the oil levels as it was company policy. So, they checked under the bonnet and took the dipstick out, which was dry. It was so dry it took over a litre of oil to get the oil level to register on the dipstick. It's always better to always check yourself. The last thing you want is to break down on the motorway and have to be rescued on the hard shoulder or worse still in a live lane, in the rain, with the traffic passing at high speed. A handy checklist can be found in Appendix 6.

One of the most important safety features on your car, that is vital you do a daily check on is your tyres, I don't mean check the pressures every day, but just look at them before you get in the car, get into the habit of walking around your car each time you get it to it, you might spot a flat tyre before you start driving rather than face the embarrassment of driving through a busy supermarket car park with a flat. Most tyre checks should be done weekly (depending on what mileage you do, but at least do these checks regularly) they should comprise tyre pressures, tread and damage. Other checks such as wheel alignment and rotating your tyres is best left to the professionals. The starting point would be your driving, skilled, controlled smooth driving will save your tyres from unnecessary wear and tear. Your tyres can lose pressure naturally over time, if you drive on an under inflated tyre this will increase your fuel consumption and lead to greater tyre wear on the outside edges, this damage to your tyres can put you at greater risk of losing control or having a blowout. An over inflated tyre will increase the wear and tear to the centre of the tyre and can also increase your risk of losing control. If your tyre is losing air quickly and you have to keep inflating it, you may have a small puncture or the value may be faulty, get your local garage or tyre expert to check this for you.

Even if your car is fitted with its own pressure monitoring system, it is still better to check them using a reliable pressure gauge which is readily available. All cars and tyres are different so consult your handbook for your car, most cars will have a plate somewhere on the bodywork that also gives you this information.

I have had a few pupils' mis-hear what I have said that I have laughed at. I once passed a steakhouse and said 'mmm steak'. She thought I had said 'mistake' and asked me after a few seconds as to what she had done wrong.

Nathan Carter - Liverpool

Roundabouts and keep clears – how do you give instruction?

I have heard of many jokes associated with our profession, and the tale I am about to tell really happened. I was asked by a close friend to teach his son to drive. It was pointed out that the lad may take a while to grasp the rudiments but was highly intelligent, just like his father. I accepted the challenge and soon found that the bond of friendship can be tested when you take on such endeavours.

In the fourth lesson I found out my car runs quite well at 5000 revs regardless of the gear we are in. I also noted that any direction is taken in a literal sense, for example, "To assist with steering you will need to pass the wheel from one hand to other" (a comment made while travelling along a country road) 'NOT NOW' I found myself saying as we instantly turned the wheel to our left, narrowly missing the hedgerow. By lesson eight we had mastered some degree of gear changes, I still felt it prudent to keep things simple, I pulled over at the roadside to explain the intricacies of roundabouts, using the clock face system I explained that we approach the roundabout at the 6 o'clock position to turn right we leave by the third exit on a standard four exit roundabout (just like the one near my students' home). Our lessons are usually at 5 pm for an hour. In the lesson, I explained the roundabouts we were approaching, the roundabout near the lad's home. We arrived and sat waiting to turn right, we sat at the junction for a while, the traffic cleared, and we still did not make any progress onto the roundabout, I wondered if he was nervous, but the look on his face was full of concentration and alertness. After what seemed several minutes but in reality, was only a minute, I enquired why we were not making progress onto the roundabout, the reply was obvious as he looked at his watch he said

"You said we approach the roundabout at 6 o'clock. It's only 5.55 pm and I was waiting for the time to join the traffic".

A valuable lesson to all PDI's and us all, the client is never wrong perhaps on occasion misguided but be careful what you say and how you say it.

Mike Yeomans – Hull

Chapter 12

Fact or Fiction

Who doesn't like a bit of myth busting?

I thought I would take this opportunity to clear up some common facts or fiction statements I hear almost daily. So, in no particular order...

- **Dual carriageways have two lanes.**

For a road to be called a dual carriageway, it must have a physical divide, a central reservation of some description. Having two lanes in one direction and two lanes in the other direction does not make a dual carriageway. If the traffic is separated by a line of paint, no matter what colour the paint is, you are on a single carriageway. It is really important that you recognise when you are on a dual carriageway or on a single carriageway if you are in a national speed limit area. This is because the limit on a national speed limit dual carriageway for cars is 70mph and on a single carriageway it's 60mph for cars.

- **Dual carriageways speed limits are all above 30mph.**

Dual carriageways can be anything from 20mph up to 70mph; being on one has very little to do with what the speed limit is, so keep looking for signs. Remember, if there are streetlights and no repeater signs you will be on a 30mph road.

- **It's okay to break the speed limit in order to overtake.**

There are no exceptions to breaking the speed limit. Exceeding the speed limit when overtaking breaks the first consideration when overtaking. If someone is already going the speed limit, then there is no need to overtake. There may be times when a critical safety incident occurs, where you may be forced to take action, these incidents should be rare. On a dual carriageway the overtaking lane exists so that you can overtake at your own pace without rushing.

- **Everybody speeds.**

No, they don't, this is a sweeping statement that people who speed used to justify their actions, because it makes them feel better. Speeding can cause collisions or incidents, and if you are caught speeding, you will get points on your licence, or be invited to attend The National Speed Awareness Course. Thankfully, speeding is now largely viewed as anti-social. So, hopefully, new drivers may no longer fall into this trap. The truth here is that everybody 'can' speed, because it's a habit. The habit being that they get used to doing 5mph over any speed limit. If you hit a pedestrian while doing 40mph as opposed to 30mph this more than quadruples your chances of killing them instantly. That they stepped out in front of your car is not your fault, but the speed you have chosen to do is. Some people say they just go with the flow, but the only flow we will stay with is the one that is fast enough for us. We won't stay with a flow that we feel is too slow. See the diagram in Appendix 8.

- **My car won't do 30mph.**

I've heard this more than you think on speed awareness courses. If this was true how on earth do these people navigate around car parks? What people are really saying here is that their car does not do 30mph on an empty road in top gear. This comes from the old way people were taught to drive, we were taught to get up into fourth gear as soon as possible. (Yes, we did only have four gears and some people might remember cars only having three!) So, some older drivers have ended up with the habit of rushing through the gears instead of using them efficiently. Cars are different nowadays. Some cars need to be in fourth gear for 30mph, others you need to be in third for 30mph. Know your car and select the correct gear for the speed. We need to make speeding as socially unacceptable as drinking and driving is now. Back in the 60s drink driving was socially acceptable, in fact you were often offered 'one for the road'. It is only now, with more education and more people who can see it makes sense not to drink and drive, that countless lives have been saved. The only way to make this happen is by people making the choice to stick to the speed limit, and drive within the laws of the road. Once people do this, others will naturally follow. But this has to start with somebody, so if not you, then who? If not now, when?

- **Motorways have slow lanes and fast lanes.**

This myth is often upheld by TV news reporters too, when they say there has been a collision on the slow lane. Motorways have a 70mph speed limit across all lanes unless otherwise stated, for cars, vans (not exceeding 7.5 tonnes maximum laden weight) buses, minibuses and motorbikes. It's 60mph if you are towing anything, driving an articulated vehicle or a heavy goods vehicle, over 7.5 tonnes maximum laden weight. The slow lane people talk about seems to be lane one or the nearside left lane. The fast lanes are allegedly lane three and four, or the far-right lanes. On a motorway there is only ONE driving lane, which is lane one, all the other lanes are for overtaking only. Once you have overtaken, you must move back into lane one or to the lane on your left, if you are overtaking a queue of slower moving vehicles then it is fine to stay in your lane, but not if the lane to the left of you is clear. Specialist officer police motorways, so speed detection technology is the favoured method. Unmarked police vehicles patrol the motorway network fitted with both video and ANPR. Static ANPR cameras work in conjunction with speed cameras that are fitted with high-definition cameras which are used to identify the driver. There is more detailed information on speed limits in Appendix 9 and 11.

- **You are allowed to exceed the speed limit by 10% plus two**

This myth may have been true many years ago because there was a time where speedometers were not that accurate. Speedometers are far more accurate now and the police can have a zero-tolerance policy whenever they like, this was at one time put in place in North Wales. As far as I am aware, the 10% plus two is still in the Association of Chief Police Officers guidelines (ACPO), since 2015 ACPO have been called the National Police Chiefs Council (NPCC), so they can still give you a tolerance if they want to. However, each police service can have a different tolerance, it is simply at the discretion of the police service so as always, just stick to the speed limit.

- **You are allowed up to 80mph on the motorway.**

No, there is a 70mph maximum speed limit on motorways. In fact, the maximum limit is there for you to do when it is safe, it is not a minimum. This myth may have come from police officers not giving chase if they see someone doing 80mph on a motorway. In many cases the police are waiting specifically for someone or something to pass, so cannot stop you. Besides, there are more and more automatic detection cameras on motorways, and the traffic police car is fitted with Closed-Circuit Television (CCTV) and Automatic Number Plate Recognition (ANPR), so you don't have to be stopped to be caught speeding on the motorway. If you choose to break the speed limit, they may eventually catch you.

- **The modern car will save me from death.**

(See Appendix 4 for the latest published road safety figures and fatalities).

Modern cars are designed to crumple in the event of a collision, even at low speeds. This is so that the body of the car absorbs the energy of the collision, and if the airbags deploy these will shield you from hitting the inside of the car, as you might already know airbags are designed to work in conjunction with the seat belts, not instead of, see point 10 below. Without a doubt, the modern car is much safer than cars of even ten years ago. But can it save you from death? No, that is impossible. When the car hits something, everything inside the car keeps going at the same speed as the car was going when it stopped abruptly. This includes your internal organs. I won't go into the gory details, but you can find more information in Appendix 9.

You can check the rating of a car before you buy one by checking the European NCAP rating. Which gives cars a star rating from zero to five. The overall safety rating was introduced in 2009 based on these four important areas.

- Adult Occupant Protection (for the driver and passenger)
- Child Occupant Protection
- Pedestrian Protection which has been expanded to include cyclists and is now known as Vulnerable Road User (VRU) protection
- Safety Assist, which evaluated driver-assistance and crash-avoidance technologies.

An overall star rating was introduced in 1997 which gave more flexibility to the ratings.

These are the official descriptions given on the Euro NCAP website.

- **5-star safety**: Overall excellent performance in crash protection and well equipped with comprehensive and robust crash avoidance technology
- **4-star safety**: Overall good performance in crash protection and all round; additional crash avoidance technology may be present
- **3-star safety**: At least average occupant protection but not always equipped with the latest crash avoidance features
- **2-star safety**: Nominal crash protection but lacking crash avoidance technology
- **1-star safety**: Marginal crash protection and little in the way of crash avoidance technology
- **0-star safety**: Meeting type-approval standards so can legally be sold but lacking critical modern safety technology

In 2021 the Polestar 2 Long Range Dual Motor, LHD, had the best rating and the Dacia Logan had the lowest. And no, I don't recognise these makes either.

- **You don't have to wear a seatbelt if you have airbags.**

It's surprising how many people still say this. It's the law to wear your seatbelt when you are in a moving vehicle, and I can't see that ever-changing. Airbags and seatbelts work together. In fact, not wearing a seatbelt in a car with airbags can cause a serious injury, if not death. Airbags inflate at approximately 200mph and most take about a 20th of a second to inflate fully. Contact with an airbag before or at the point of full inflation can cause death, it would be like hitting your face against a brick wall, at speed. Seatbelts are now fitted with pretensioners, this is where the seat belt pulls you back into your seat, and part of their job is to hold you back in your seat until the airbag is past the point of full inflation.

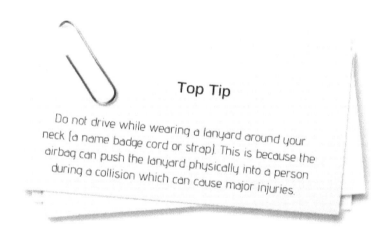

Top Tip

Do not drive while wearing a lanyard around your neck (a name badge cord or strap). This is because the airbag can push the lanyard physically into a person during a collision which can cause major injuries.

There is a link in Appendix 9 where you can find more out about seatbelt law and the exemptions.

- **Anti-Lock Braking System (ABS) will stop your car from skidding.**

You can still skid with ABS. ABS allows you to steer and brake hard at the same time. During emergency braking, the wheels of a car that are not fitted with ABS, will simply lock up, so the driver cannot steer.

On cars with ABS, when the ABS system kicks in, the car might feel like it is jumping about a little, for me it feels and sounds like I am stopping over gravel, this is the sound of the system working. Not every car reacts the same, so it is a good idea to try the system out in your own car, but only when it is 100% safe to do, maybe in a large, empty car park.

The reason you can still skid with ABS is that the friction of the tyres on the road will eventually stop the car. Meaning if the tyre condition is poor or the road surface is slippery or loose, then you can still skid.

- **ABS stop you quicker.**

ABS allow you to break and steer at the same time. A car fitted with ABS can actually take longer to stop. For example, if the surface is loose due to gravel, snow or sand it will take much longer as the ABS system stops the wheels from digging in, instead the car will bounce along the top of the surface.

- **20mph speed limits are only enforced when the schools are open.**

All mandatory speed limits can be enforced 24/7, 365 days a year. (A mandatory speed limit will have a red circle around the number, if there is no red circle it is an advisory limit) Some police services around the country are enforcing these speed limits and used to offer a 20mph speed awareness course. This course is now no longer offered, instead people who are caught speeding in a 20mph speed limit or 20mph zone are offered the normal National Speed Awareness Course.

A few years ago, I parked on the side of a 20mph city centre road, chatting to a driving instructor I was training, when we spotted two mounted police officers that were riding behind us, and a car came speeding past, which almost shook our car. They must have spotted the mounted police officers as they tried to slow down, but the officers flagged them down and promptly wrote them a ticket. While I can't say exactly what that ticket was for, the moral of the story remains, just stick to the speed limits.

From 2018 the 20mph speed awareness course amalgamated into the National Speed Awareness Course, and I meet about three to four people a month who have been caught on a 20mph road, and I am just one of the many speed awareness trainers around the country. I have heard some drivers say the 20mph is far too slow, but, too slow for who?

- **Speed cameras don't contain film.**

Well, this is difficult, because sometimes they do, and sometimes they don't. They removed the early speed cameras from their housing or yellow box from one to another, because there wasn't enough money to put a speed camera in every yellow housing. Sometimes a camera will run out of film. Today, more and more cameras are digital, so it's more likely these days that a speed camera box or housing, is holding a fully functioning camera.

In 2018 the Red Speed cameras, now called 'Speed on Green' were introduced in Merseyside. These cameras will detect anyone who crosses the white line after the red stop light comes on. However, they will also catch anyone who is speeding through the green light. They also use these cameras in other parts of the country. Remember, a collision at a traffic light junction can be serious as it is likely both vehicles were speeding up, one beating the lights, the other moving off quickly. You have been warned. Statistics, according to The Royal Society for the Prevention of Accidents (RoSPA) show collisions are reduced where there is a camera. The number of people killed or seriously injured fell by 42% at camera sites. I have included a link in Appendix 9.

- **The speed camera has run out of film.**

See point 14 above. As I mentioned most cameras are digital now, and digital never runs out, never needs to get changed and runs 24/7. The old GATSO cameras sometimes run out of film, there is also a high cost involved with running and the upkeep of these older cameras because they run on wet film, this has to be replaced and they have to have the staff to replace them.

- **Built-up areas are always 30mph speed limits.**

Many built-up areas are indeed 30mph speed limits. However, a built-up area when we are looking at speed limits, is any road with street lights on, except motorways of course. Depending on what type of road it is and what historical risk data there is for that road in the built-up area, means that there may be many speed limits enforced, now often they are 20mph. Residential areas and near schools often have 20mph limits. There is now a big push to have a blanket 20mph on all residential and city centre roads, this is because there is less than 1% chance of killing someone instantly if they are hit at 20mph. See Appendix 8 and for the latest data on this is in the resources section in Appendix 9.

Anyway, back to the question, there are built-up areas without a single building, they are built-up areas because they have streetlights. (*I like to call them speedlights, 30mph speedlights*) The highway code states if there are streetlights it is 30mph unless otherwise stated.

To sum up again, as it is important, a built-up area is any road with streetlights. In a nutshell, it's the streetlights that mark it as a built-up area, not the buildings. For example, in an industrial area many of the roads are 30mph, this allows heavy goods drivers enough time to exit a side road or property safely and with ease, they simply need more space and time to manoeuvre the vehicle out into the traffic.

- **Speed awareness courses are just money-making.**

Funnily enough, people often quote this myth when attending the actual speed awareness course. It is far from the truth. In many areas, the payment made for courses is cheaper than the speeding fine. The speed awareness courses also carry a cost, most of the money goes towards room hire and refreshments (if you get any,) trainer fees, stationary, administration and insurance to name just a few. In the COVID-19 pandemic the courses where offered digitally, so that people still had this choice, but although you had to get your own coffee and there was no room hire to pay for, the on-line platforms had to be paid for, the back office staff, the trainers and of course a full technical team there to help people get on to the course or help the trainers with any difficulties they were having. So, why would someone create a business model with so many costs; when simply sending out a speeding fine is far easier, and probably gains more money? Instead of a money-making exercise The National Speed Awareness Course exists to offer people a chance to change their attitude and behaviour about speeding or to just simply think about it. We all need to agree that it is morally and legally right to travel within the speed limit and make speeding socially unacceptable, just like drink driving. There are people we share the road with whom feel it is totally acceptable to break or bend the rules of the road. I cannot think of another set of rules and regulations where this happens, for example, if it was a sport, a hobby, a procedure at work or health and safety rules, we would not be encouraging people to break or bend the rules however it seems to happen with the rules of the road. If you are someone who feels they have a right to break the speed limit with no penalty, then those who stick to the speed limit have the right to do this too.

Top Tip

Keep in third gear for the 30 zones, we no longer teach learners to get up into the highest gear as quickly as possible, we teach them to be in the gear that will give them the most control (if your vehicle is happy in this gear)

Any surplus money from speed awareness courses is donated to the Road Safety Trust for local road safety initiatives. One local initiative the Merseyside Road Safety Partnership undertook was offering free driving assessments for the over 60's. More information on UKROEd which is the private not-for-profit company that conducts the management and administration of the National Driver Offender Retraining Schemes (NDORS) on behalf of the Police service, can be found in Appendix 9.

- **All speed cameras have to be painted yellow.**

At the time of publishing many permanent traffic enforcement cameras are painted yellow, however, not all traffic cameras are permanent, some are handheld, and these are not yellow. Also, please note that not all fixed cameras are painted yellow either, the ones that are yellow, are in that colour in order to stand out and help you, the driver. You should see the yellow camera housing in plenty of time which gives you time to make sure you are not speeding. There is a school of thought that if drivers slow down too quickly, the camera can create a dangerous situation. While this happens, it isn't the cameras' fault; it is the drivers' fault for speeding in the first place, coupled with a lack of observation. If they were not speeding, they would not have been forced to slow down so quickly. Also, some people claim police officers undertaking speed enforcement hide in bushes, this is simply not the case. People just see the police officer very late and don't have time to slow down, some people don't even see them at all and wonder how they got caught speeding. But ask yourself this, if you are happy to slow down when you see a speed camera or the police, you must know you are speeding. There are a minority of drivers who will flash other cars to warn them of an impending speed camera, this is illegal, as it is perverting the course of justice, which can result in a prison sentence. Often on speed awareness courses I hear people complaining that the police are out there to 'catch them!' My response is, 'catch you doing what?' I have put a link in Appendix 9 giving you the top 10 tips to stay within the speed limit.

Having been in the industry for quite some time, and clearly, there will be more than one story to use here, my thoughts on this story are based on my return to work from one very long lockdown due to the pandemic.

I wanted to start my return to work very slowly, mainly, as I definitely would be rusty and secondly, I wanted to be able to really focus on each learner, more so now due to the time off we all have had.
We had a training situation occur during a lesson. It happened upon entering a car park that was quite busy. We approached a very faded zebra crossing. The learner noticed it - no problem. The learner also noticed that there was a lady with a trolley already on the crossing.

So, my learner pulled up safely and waited. All good ... until the lady started to shout, "Go on, you can go". My learner looked at me and said "I can't go can I?" (we are both wearing face masks in this story) I replied with "Why?" "What are the rules" and so on. Meanwhile, the lady continued to shout "Go on! Move!" so we sat there shaking our heads and continued with questions on safety etc. I also asked the learner whilst waiting, to look into the trolley to look for clues. This could be why the lady keeps asking us to drive on. This is the important part of the story here. We will come back to the trolley later.

So, whilst all this was going on, a man shouted, "They can't love. You need to cross as they are in a lesson. She's trying to teach the learner there" and with that, the lady decided to start walking across. However, it was clear now that the lady was struggling to walk, using the trolley as an aid.

Once the crossing was clear, the learner drove on and found a suitable place to park to discuss. So, I began by saying "Remember the trolley? Can you tell me what was in the trolley, that gave you a clue as to why the pedestrian wanted you to drive on over the crossing?" The learner had a think and said, "Bog roll!" I turned to look at the learner to see what led the learner to think the clue was toilet rolls. The learner looked very impressed. Even though the learner was still wearing the mask, the learner looked completely chuffed. I should have to ask why? The response I got was "Well, you asked me to be observant to look for clues. The lady looked like she was struggling to walk, and I saw the bog rolls, and thought, ``God bless her, she's desperate for the loo!"

I looked on, not knowing how to react. Indeed, the learner looked so impressed, I knew if I had burst out laughing, then it may have offended them. So, I tried to remain professional and instead went for the positive approach of "Very good on your observation skills there. I was indeed hoping you had seen the aids in the trolley? No? There were a pair of crutches and therefore the lady was hoping we would drive past her so that she could indeed take her time rather than feeling rushed across the crossing".

I guess we both learnt something that day… be careful how you word things or be ready for a completely different answer!

Leanne Condliff Liverpool

A pupil asked if he was driving a Ford Fiesta, my response was 'Focus'. He thought I was telling him off with this being his first lesson and I only realised when there was an uncomfortable silence. He then realised I meant 'Ford Focus'.

Nathan Carter - Liverpool

Chapter 13

What Gets in the Way of Good Driving?

Everyone has the skill and ability to drive well, in fact, anyone can keep any vehicle at any speed over any distance on any road, all you have to do is stick a police car behind them, then suddenly it's hands at ten to two, keep checking my mirrors, and make sure I signal this time. Go on, you know I am right!

I know it is not just speed that drivers often get wrong but if you enjoy driving fast and want high-speed fun, then get out on the track. Search the internet for track days and you will find something close to you. Apparently, only 18% of drivers like driving really fast. If this is you, do it. Just make sure you do it in a controlled environment. Racing car drivers are equipped to drive fast, I know they go much faster than someone doing 36mph in a 30mph zone. However, they wear fire retardant clothing, and have a specially adapted vehicle, crash helmets, fire engines and ambulances around every bend, with no oncoming traffic, no pedestrians, although I guess the odd spectator might get in the way. Racing drivers are strapped in the car with specially adapted seats and a highly trained co-driver, so if you look at racing car drivers, they are fully prepared to crash. Whereas we are probably going to buy a pint of milk. This may only happen in Merseyside, but we often see drivers nipping to the local shops in pyjamas and slippers, not even ready for that puddle they are going to step in.

It is not the driving of the car that lets us down on the road, we test that; it's not the knowing of the rules, we test that too. It's our emotions that let us down time and time again, we don't test that. On a driving test there is one goal, to pass the test; so, we concentrate really hard and do our very best to get it right, we will endeavour to create the perfect drive.

After we pass, every time we drive, every journey will have a different goal; from getting to work on time, to picking friends up, from rushing to hospital to going on holiday, the list is endless. It is these times we can let our emotions get in the way. All we can do is to keep driving well and developing good habits.

The only negative, if there is one, is that good driving will hardly get noticed, good drivers go under the radar, no one outside your car can feel how smooth you are driving, can tell how much fuel you are saving and how well you are looking after your car. Poor driving will get everyone's attention for all the wrong reasons, we look at bad drivers and often say something like "what a complete idiot!" or something much worse. It's not what drivers 'can' do that counts, it is what drivers do when they are not being watched, which will help to make and keep our roads safe.

When asking a very well-educated girl if she'd heard of the two-second rule, she replied, "Is that when you drop food on the floor? I told her she was too posh as that was five seconds in my house.

Antonia Louise Naylor - Whitby/Ellesmere Port

Afterword

How COVID-19 Affected the Driving Instructor Industry 2020

It's a real shame to end this book on such a negative subject, but I simply have to write something on how COVID-19 has affected our industry.

Driving instructors all over the country suffered both financial and mental hardship, although there were some whose financial situation lent itself to them having an extended holiday. During the first lockdown in early March 2020, we were allowed to take critical workers for lessons and driving tests, although this still carried risks of the driving instructors catching COVID-19 or passing it on to their families.

There were hundreds of instructors who had not long started their businesses. Unfortunately, they were excluded from any government financial help, most of them had to rely on Universal Credit if they could get that.

We were allowed to teach again, with restrictions, in mid-July 2020, after the first lockdown. Sadly, this was short-lived, and we were off the road again in November 2020 because of the new tier system.

Finally, in December 2020 we were back teaching, but unfortunately, in January 2021, the country went into lockdown and the driving instructors were unable to earn any money once again.

Instructors had to fight to get some financial help from their local councils as they were not on the official list of businesses forced to close because of COVID-19. It was my view that we were forced to close, the DVSA told us we must not give driving lessons and clarified that if anybody taught lessons during this time, they could have their licence to teach removed.

Finally, at the time of publication, we were allowed to go back in April 2021 again hoping that we could remain working and earning money, supporting our families and becoming emotionally stable again.

Sadly, some driving instructors lost their lives to COVID-19 during this pandemic including some instructors I had trained, may they all rest in peace, my thoughts still go out to their families.

There were also many instructors who simply decided enough was enough and stopped teaching altogether, some went into retirement, some got different jobs which they enjoyed and never came back. Some trainee instructors gave up becoming instructors because of the uncertainty of the lockdowns.

I believe we lost a lot of great driving instructors during this awful time.

Independent driving instructors were on their own during this challenging time apart from the local instructors I know, who supported each other by sharing information, humorous stories and pictures, anything just to keep everybody going via WhatsApp.

Instructors working with driving schools on a franchise had a mixture of positive and negative experiences. Some schools still wanted to charge their instructors either their full franchise fees or a retainer fee. One national driving school allegedly paused the franchise payments so after the pandemic was over that money was still owed to the company by the instructors, putting them into debt. All I can say is that at Insight 2 Drive we immediately stopped all franchise payments from our instructors and we continued to support them. We arranged regular on-line meetings twice a week, one was a business meeting where we heard guest speakers from the ADINJC, FSB, accountants, coaches, financial advisors, GDPR specialists, financial planning, marketing. The other one was more of a social get together. We would organise a quiz, our own version of Catchphrase, Scattergories and we learned how to play poker.

Most of the Insight 2 Drive instructors also underwent online training for the control of infectious diseases, which the company offered to pay for.

At the end of the first lockdown when we thought it was all over Insight 2 Drive provided all their driving instructors with a 'welcome back to work pack' it comprised of hand sanitiser, gloves, masks, leaflets on helping to keep the car COVID free, jokes, riddles, a thank-you card and of course their favourite chocolate bar.

Here are some comments from some of our instructors on how COVID-19 has affected them.

★ *My comment is brief, in fact here you go. Fatter, mild alcoholic and semi-mental -* **Andy Keywood Insight 2 Drive.**

★ *The Covid-19 period has disrupted both my job as a driving instructor and our life. The long periods of time away from the job has meant that we have had to start and stop lessons which has affected the service to our pupils and also had a financial impact on my business. I have been a driving instructor since November 2018, and this meant that I did not qualify for the government SEISS grant financial support. The time away from the job has given me the opportunity to evaluate my plan and work with my children home schooling. I am now ready to start lessons again which I look forward to getting back on the road* *and helping my learners to achieve their goals. - **Kevin Gilfoyle Insight 2 Drive.***

The final word on Covid-19 comes from the ADINJC who, along with the MSA, DIA and ADI Federation, helped to support instructors all over the country by having their own online webinars keeping us all up to date on the very fast changing world we lived in.

★ "As a leading national association for driving instructors, we never imagined initially how much impact the pandemic in 2020-2021 would have on the industry. However, it became obvious that it was a major issue because it effectively stopped the majority of driver training and testing. We knew we needed to step up and help our members and the industry. Instructors were not only hit financially but also on a personal and emotional level that left many of them quite desperate. We introduced extra phone lines and communication streams apart from our usual helpline, we ran a business line and a talk line where there was always a willing person to listen and lend support to instructors. Getting information out quickly was vital so we could keep the industry as up to date as possible and we helped with a COVID toolkit of support and useful guides. The zoom platform became vital not only for us to hold webinars and to get facts and messages out but to help with training whilst instructors had time away from work. Our help and support were much appreciated by the industry from the feedback we received. ADINJC has always risen to any challenges since it was founded in 1973 and this one will be remembered for a long time and it will take many years to recover from it." - ***Lynne Barrie MA, ADINJC Chair.***

Appendix 1

My CPD Journey - Kathy Higgins

Awards

- Nominated for EVAS 10th Anniversary Enterprise Vision Awards 2021
- Shortlisted for the Intelligent Instructor Awards 2021
- Global Business Insight Recognised Leader in Driving Teaching Servicers 2019
- Nominated for Best Business Enabler with National Entrepreneur Awards 2015
- Nominated for Best Business Video with National Entrepreneur Awards 2015

- Nominated for Best Customer Service with National Entrepreneur Awards 2015
- Nominated for Best Business Enabler with National Entrepreneur Awards 2015
- Nominated for Best use of New Media with National Entrepreneur Awards 2015
- Winner of the Enterprise Vision Award in Training and Coaching category 2014
- Highly Commended runner up of the Enterprise Vision Award - 2013
- Presented with the ADINJC contribution to CPD Award 2013
- Winner of the Golden L Award for the favourite local franchise 2013
- Winner of the BNI Givers Gain Award – 2011
- BNI Notable Networker Award for outstanding performance awarded for outstanding contribution in 2011
- BNI Notable Networker Award for outstanding performance awarded for outstanding contribution in 2011(second award)
- Winner of the Women in Business Best Networker Award – 2008
- Shortlisted for the FSB British Small Business Champions –2008
- Winner of the Merseyside Women Making a difference Award – 2005
- Awarded the Kelly Elite Award by Kelly Temporary Services 1989

Membership of Professional Bodies

- Association of Industrial Road Safety Officers – now called The Association 4 Road Risk Management (ARM)
- BRAKE – the road safety charity
- Master drivers Club
- ADI Federation
- The Women's Organisation
- Young Enterprise
- Guild of Experienced Motorists
- Engage Instructor for Cheshire & Merseyside
- Institute of Master Tutors of Driving *(Secretary)*
- Master Drivers Club with the DIA
- Federation of small businesses *(Liverpool & Knowsley Committee member)*
- RoSPA - Advanced Drivers Association *(Diploma Holder)*
- Driving Instructors Association *(Diamond test examiner)*
- Approved Driving Instructors National Joint Council *(served on the committee)*
- Motor Schools Association *(Served on the NW Committee)*
- Institute of Advanced Motorists

Career Development

- UKROEd - Understanding Attitudes & Behaviours
- ITQ level 2 Certificate

- UKROEd - Behaviour Change Interventions (accredited paper cert)
- UKROEd - Achieving Excellence in Virtual Training
- Criminology and Profiling Course
- UKROEd - Internal Monitoring Workshop
- Road Safety GB - The Ageing Driver ADI Training Course
- DriveTech Ltd - started at Trainer Development Coach, part time to support NDORS trainers delivering courses online
- UKROEd - Supporting ESOL Clients
- Virtual Collage - Prevent COVID-19
- AA Driving School - COVID-19 e-training module
- UKROEd - Diversity & Inclusion Course
- Highfield eLearning - Infection Prevention and Control COVID-19 e-training
- Engage Partnership Driving Instructor Seminar
- IAM Roadsmart - I achieved the IAM First. To celebrate 25 years of advanced driving in February
- ADINJC - Standards Check Workshop
- UW - Team Leader promotion
- RoSPA Advanced Drivers and Riders Diploma - Pass
- RoSPA Advanced driving re-test at Diploma Level - Pass
- Adult Mental Health First Aid (Welsh) with Training in Mind
- NDORS National Speed Awareness Instructor Course 2-day instructors' course with Dr Fiona Fylan

- NDORS Safe and Considerate Driving and WDU Instructor Course 2-day instructors' course with Dr Simon Christmas
- Road Safety GB - Client Centred Learning Certificate award
- Diamond Elite Test - Pass
- Road Safety Conference with Graham Feest
- Client Centred Learning course with Ian Edwards - Two-day workshop
- UW College of Excellence - Team Building Workshop
- Getting the best from your PDIs - One-day workshop with Louise Walsh
- Awarded the Fellowship of the Institute of Master Tutors of Driving (IMTD)
- Royal Society for the Prevention of Accidents RoADA retest - Pass
- Drug, Solvent & Alcohol Abuse Counselling Level 4 with Stonebridge Associated Colleges
- NDORS 2017 - Train the Trainer Annual Training Day
- NADIP - Enhanced Communication five-hour workshop by Nick Looby
- UW - Certificate of Achievement promotion
- TTC - NDORS Training Course for the National Speed Awareness Course
- DVSA Standards Test - Grade A
- Royal Society for the Prevention of Accidents RoADA retest - Pass

- NVQ Assessors Award to deliver BTEC Level 1 and 2
- Pearson Edexcel Level 3 in Assessing Vocational Achievement with AnyDriver
- Pearson EDI Certificate in Functional Skills in Mathematics
- Pearson EDI Certificate in Functional Skills qualification in English
- Driving 4 Change - driver psychology course
- HeartStart - Emergency Life Support course with Insight 2 Drive
- Solving Problems through Speaking and Listening - Level 2
- Improving your Listening Skills - Level 2 with ALS Liverpool
- Solving Problems through Speaking and Listening - Level 1
- Improving Trainer Excellence through feedback and self-evaluation on behalf of Drivesafe
- Balancing Act - Equality and Diversity delivered by Wavelength Social Marketing CIC
- RoSPA Diploma retest - Pass
- Roadcraft and Police Advanced Driving Techniques with Chris Gilbert of Driving Tomorrow
- Training Monitor Driving Theory Ltd - online training course
- What's Driving Us by Dr Fiona Fylan - two-day training course
- Psychological Approaches to Driver Education - One-day course with Ian Edwards
- BTEC (Level 4) Professional Award in Coaching for Driver Development

- L of a way to Pass - TFT Half-day workshop exploring the use of Thought Field Therapy for special needs learners
- Revolution's course - with Julia Malkin MBE Learning how to teach people on the Autistic Spectrum
- Improving Learning Through Self-evaluation - Ian Edwards course
- Engage learner centred training course
- ORDIT (Official Register of Driving Instructor Trainers) renewal
- National Driver Alertness Trainers Course
- Introduction to Enterprise Mentoring Certificate by Get Mentoring
- Executive Business Coach with the International Coaching Academy, accredited with the Institute of Leadership and Management
- Royal Society for the Prevention of Accidents RoADA retest - Pass
- Personal Performance Coach with the International Coaching Academy
- Liverpool Conference for Driving Instructors - How to reach your goals and build a premiership business
- BNI Director Training - Launching Chapters
- Corporate Manslaughter Workshop with Ged Latham
- Accelerated Learning with the International Coaching Academy
- Coaching and the GDE Matrix workshop with AAdrivetech

- Equality 2010 workshop with AAdrivetech
- University of East London - Coaching for Driver Development
- ORDIT Straight 6's in an ORDIT inspection, (Official Register of Driving Instructor Trainers)
- Merseyside Police Driver Training - Advanced ADI Commentary Course
- Hope University - Business Programme 8-week evening course
- Check Test Grade six given in a Fleet Check Test
- Alert Driving - Hazard Perception Evaluation online course
- DriveSafe, National Driver Alertness Training Course
- DriveSafe - Traffic Light Awareness Training Course
- DriveSafe - National Speed Awareness Training Course
- Teaching & Assessment Skills with John Farlam
- PTTLS Preparing to Teach in the Lifelong Learning Sector
- Post Graduate Certificate in Coaching for Driver Development with the University of East London
- TTC - Speed Awareness National Model Training Course
- TTC - Speed Awareness National Model Training (Theory) Course
- Training Solutions - Emergency First Aid
- Brake & FedEx Road Safety Academy Graduate - Company Driver Programme
- Mentor Corporate Coaching - Results Centred Leadership Programme
- DriveSafe - NSAC Training course

- Royal Society for the Prevention of Accidents RoADA retest - Pass
- Certificate of Skid Control with the National Car Control Centre
- DIAmond - Accredited Taxi-driver Trainer Course
- ORDIT Registered Trainer
- AIM Instructor Training with Phil Hirst
- ADINJC - How to Become a Successful ADI
- Skid Car (UK) - Tutors Course in Skid Control
- Edexcel BTEC - Diploma in Driving Instruction Advanced
- Fleet Check Test Grade 5
- RoSPA - Occupational Advanced Driving Test - Pass
- IAM Special Assessment - Pass
- Department of Transport Safe and Fuel-Efficient Driving SAFED trainers' course
- RoSPA Advanced Retest - Pass
- Managing Occupational Road Risk Course
- Royal Society for the Prevention of Accidents RoADA retest - Pass
- DIA Advanced Examiner for the DIAmond Advanced Test
- DIAmond Advanced Examiner course with the DIA
- IAM Driving Assessment for Advanced Driving - Pass
- Hazard Perception Test - Pass
- DSA Cardington Special Test - Pass
- DIAmond Advanced Special Test - Pass
- DriveTech Induction course - Pass

- RAC Advanced Test - Pass
- Skills for the ADI Trainer by John Farlam
- LDC - Group teaching workshop
- RoSPA Advanced driving test passed at Gold standard
- Driving Services - 'Train the trainer' course
- Official Register of Driving Instructor Training
- Diploma in Driving Instruction
- Royal Society for the Prevention of Accidents passed at Silver Standard
- DIAmond Advanced Motorist - Pass
- Marie Curie Ladies driving Challenge
- DSA ADI, Qualified Driving instructor
- LCCI Examination Board NVQ level 3 in Owner Management and Business Planning
- Selling for Professionals with Catalyst Training & Development
- Institute of Advanced Motorists IAM test - Pass

Appendix 2

Photo of Instructor

Instructors ADI Number

ADI Registrar's signature

Valid Between dates

This side will be visible from the inside of the window screen

This side will be visible from the outside of the window screen

The Certificate is LIGHT GREEN

The size of the certificate is approx 10cms square and is coated in plastic

The Expiry Date

This is what a Trainee
licence looks like.

This side will be visible
from the inside of the
window screen

This side will be visible
from the outside of the
window screen

It is PINK in colour and has
the same information as
the ADI Certifcatte above

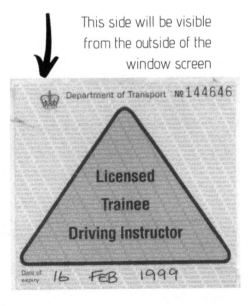

Other certificates will look like this, although on the ORDIT and the Fleet badge the DSA logo is no longer used.

The ORDIT certificate is pink with the octagonal shape on the right side.

The fully qualified ADI badge is green with the octagonal shape on the reverse side.

This is a Fleet Driver Trainer certificate. It is beige with the octagonal shape on the reverse side.

The ORDIT and the Fleet Certificates are vocational certificates.

Appendix 3

Illegal Driving Instructor Poster – Download Your Free Copy

https://insight2drive.co.uk/an-insight-to-drive-the-book/

Appendix 4

Reported Road Casualties in Great Britain 2019

Updated every September.

- People Killed - **1,752** - *As reported to the police* - (**39** of these were children).
- People seriously injured (unadjusted) - **25,945.**
- People seriously injured (adjusted) - **30,144.**
- KSI (unadjusted) - **27,697** - *KSI - People killed or seriously injured.*
- KSI (adjusted) - **31,896.**
- People slightly injured (unadjusted) - **125,461.**
- People slightly injured (adjusted) - **121,262.**
- **All casualties - 153,158.**

Adjusted estimates from the Office for National Statistics Methodology Advisory Service.

Fatalities by road user type

736 people killed in cars.

470 pedestrians killed.

336 bikers killed.

100 cyclists killed.

110 other people killed (not in the groups above).

Updated information can be found here;

https://www.gov.uk/government/collections/road-accidents-and-safety-statistics

Or downloaded from;

https://insight2drive.co.uk/an-insight-to-drive-the-book/

Appendix 5

Your examiner will ask you one question from the 'tell me' section. This will happen at the start of your test, before you start driving. You need to explain what you would do.

While you are driving, you will be asked one 'show me' question and you will have to carry out the task safely. If both answers you give are wrong (one explanation and one action) you will get you one driving fault (sometimes called a 'minor' fault).

You will fail your driving test if your driving is dangerous or potentially dangerous while you perform the action to answer the 'show me' question.

Tell Me - Questions and Answers

1. Tell me how you would check that the brakes are working before starting a journey?

Brakes should not feel spongy or slack. Test the brakes before you set off. The vehicle should not pull to one side.

2. Tell me where you would find the information for the recommended tyre pressures for this car and how tyre pressure should be checked?

Check the manufacturer's guide, use a reliable pressure gauge, check and adjust pressures when tyres are cold, don't forget the spare tyre, remember to refit the valve caps.

3. Tell me how you make sure your head restraint is adjusted correctly, so it provides the best protection in the event of a crash?

The head restraint should be adjusted so the rigid part of the head restraint is at least as high as your eye or top of your ears, and as close to the back of the head as is comfortable. Note: Some head restraints might not be adjustable.

4. Tell me how you would check the tyres to ensure that they have sufficient tread depth and that their general condition is safe to use on the road?

There should be no cuts and bulges, and 1.6mm of tread depth across the central three-quarters of the breadth of the tyre, and around the entire outer circumference of the tyre.

5. Tell me how you would check that the headlights and taillights are working? You do not need to exit the vehicle.

Explain that you would operate the switch (turn on ignition if necessary), then walk around the vehicle.

6. Tell me how you would know if there was a problem with your anti-lock braking system?

The warning light should illuminate if there is a fault with the anti-lock braking system.

7. Tell me how you would check the direction indicators are working? You do not need to exit the vehicle.

Explain that you would operate the switch (turn on ignition if necessary), and then walk around the vehicle.

8. Tell me how you would check the brake lights are working on this car?

Explain you would operate the brake pedal, make use of reflections in windows or doors, or ask someone to help.

9. Tell me how you would check if the power-assisted steering is working before starting a journey?

If the steering becomes heavy, the system may not be working properly. Before starting a journey, you need to do two simple checks. Firstly, place slight pressure on the steering wheel, maintain this while you start the engine. This should cause a slight but noticeable movement as the system operates. Alternatively, turning the steering wheel just after moving off will indicate if the power assistance is functioning or not.

10. Tell me how you would switch on the rear fog light(s) and explain when you would use it/them? You do not need to exit the vehicle.

Operate the switch (turn on dipped headlights and ignition if necessary). Check the warning light is on. Explain their use.

11. Tell me how you switch your headlight from dipped to main beam and explain how you would know the main beam is on?

Operate switch (with ignition or engine on if necessary), check that the main beam warning light is on.

12. Open the bonnet and tell me how you would check that the engine has sufficient oil?

Identify dipstick/oil level indicator, describe how you would check the oil level against the minimum and maximum markers on the dipstick.

13. Open the bonnet and tell me how you would check that the engine has sufficient engine coolant?

Identify the high-level and low-level markings on the header tank where fitted or radiator filler cap and describe how to top up to the correct level.

14. Open the bonnet and tell me how you would check that you have a safe level of hydraulic brake fluid?

Identify the reservoir, check the level against the high and low markings.

You need to open the bonnet and tell the examiner how you would do the check if you're asked question 12, 13 or 14.

Show Me - Questions and Answers

- When it is safe to do so, can you show me how you wash and clean the rear windscreen?
- When it is safe to do so, can you show me how you wash and clean the front windscreen?
- When it is safe to do so, can you show me how you would switch on your dipped headlights?
- When it is safe to do so, can you show me how you had set the rear demister?
- When it is safe to do so, can you show me how you would operate the horn?
- When it is safe to do so, can you show me how you would demist the front windscreen?
- When it is safe to do so, can you show me how you would open and close the side window?

The important words here are '**when it is safe to do so**'

Appendix 6

These three handouts can be downloaded at -

https://insight2drive.co.uk/an-insight-to-drive-the-book/

<u>Power Checks</u>

- <u>Petrol</u> – *Make sure you have enough fuel for your journey. Consider weather conditions & the load your vehicle is carrying.*

- <u>Oil</u> – *Make sure your oil is between the minimum & maximum markers on the dipstick.*

- <u>Water & Wipers</u> – *Make sure you have enough water/coolant/antifreeze. Also check windscreen washer fluid. Check windscreen wipers, both front & rear (if applicable) and make sure there are no tears in the rubber or embedded foreign objects.*

- <u>Electrics</u> – *Make sure all lights are clean and working before starting a journey. Check headlights (dipped & main beam), taillights, fog lights, brake lights, indicators & number plate lights. Check & monitor the electric warning lights on the dashboard.*

- <u>Rubber</u> – *Check all tyres (including the spare) are inflated to the correct pressures and they have a minimum of 1.6mm of tread across the central ¾ of the breadth of the tyre. Make sure there are no cuts, bulges or foreign objects and that all dust caps are in place.*

<u>Powdery Checks</u>

- <u>Petrol</u> – *Make sure you have enough fuel for your journey. Consider weather conditions & the load your vehicle is carrying.*

- <u>Oil</u> – *Make sure your oil is between the minimum & maximum markers on the dipstick.*

- <u>Water & Wipers</u> – *Make sure you have enough water/coolant/antifreeze. Also check windscreen washer fluid. Check windscreen wipers, both front & rear (if applicable) and make sure there are no tears in the rubber or embedded foreign objects.*

- Damage – *Walk around the vehicle and check for any external damage, including all lights, glass and tyres, make a note of your findings and send them to the appropriate person before you drive the car.*

- <u>Electrics</u> – *Make sure all lights are clean and working before starting a journey. Check headlights (dipped & main beam), taillights, fog lights, brake lights, indicators & number plate lights. Check & monitor the electric warning lights on the dashboard.*

- <u>Rubber</u> – *Check all tyres (including the spare) are inflated to the correct pressures and they have a minimum of 1.6mm of tread across the central ¾ of the breadth of the tyre. Make sure there are no cuts, bulges or foreign objects and that all dust caps are in place.*

Flowery Checks

- <u>Fuel</u> – *Make sure you have enough fuel for your journey. Consider weather conditions & the load your vehicle is carrying.*

- <u>Lights</u> – *Make sure all lights are clean and working before starting a journey. Check headlights (dipped & main beam), taillights, fog lights, brake lights, indicators & number plate lights.*

- <u>Oil</u> – *Make sure your oil is between the minimum & maximum markers on the dipstick.*

- <u>Water</u> – *Make sure you have enough water/coolant/antifreeze. Also check windscreen washer fluid.*

- <u>Electrics</u> – *Check & monitor the electric warning lights on the dashboard.*

- <u>Rubber</u> – *Check all tyres (including the spare) are inflated to the correct pressures and they have a minimum of 1.6mm of tread across the central ¾ of the breadth of the tyre. Check for cuts, bulges or foreign objects and that all dust caps are in place. Also check windscreen wipers, both front & rear (if applicable) and check there are no tears in the rubber or embedded foreign objects.*

- <u>Yourself</u> – *Make sure you are fit to drive. Consider previous alcohol intake, medication (both prescribed & over the counter) and state of mind. Make sure you have had sufficient rest/sleep and that you are not tired.*

Appendix 7

Driving test pass rates can be found on this website –

<u>Driving test statistics (DRT) - GOV.UK (www.gov.uk)</u>

Pass rate figures between April 2007 to September 2020.

→ The lowest pass rate was in November 2017 at 43%

→ The highest (pre COVID-19) pass rate was in September 2020 at 48%

During the national lockdown when tests were available to Key Workers, the pass rate was 61.2% in April 2020.

You can find driving centre pass rates on this website -

<u>Car driving test data by test centre - GOV.UK (www.gov.uk)</u>

April 2019 - March 2020

→ The lowest pass rate was Birmingham (The Pavilion) test centre at 28.9%.

→ The highest pass rate was the Isle of Mull at 88.2%

Appendix 8

Impact speeds

There is a comprehensive study.

https://www.RoSPA.com/RoSPAweb/docs/advice-services/road-safety/drivers/20-mph-zone-factsheet.pdf

Or downloaded as a handout;

https://insight2drive.co.uk/an-insight-to-drive-the-book/

Hit a pedestrian at 20mph and there is a 1% chance of killing them instantly or a 99% chance they would survive that impact

Hit them at 30mph and there is a 7% chance of killing them.

Hit them at 40mph and there is a 31% chance of killing them instantly.

The difference is staggering.

20mph speed limit = 1% fatality

30mph speed limit = 7% fatality

40mph speed limit = 31% fatality

Appendix 9

Resource website addresses –
https://insight2drive.co.uk/an-insight-to-drive-the-book/

- 20mph Fact sheet from RoSPA:

  www.RoSPA.com/RoSPAweb/docs/advice-services/road-safety/drivers/20-mph-zone-factsheet.pdf

- Accident and casualty costs:

  www.gov.uk/government/statistical-data-sets/ras60-average-value-of-preventing-road-accidents

- ADI Federation: https://www.theadifederation.org.uk/

- Alliance of British Drivers: https://www.abd.org.uk/

- An introduction to KROEd:

  https://ukr-resources-4.s3.eu-west-2.amazonaws.com/wp-content/uploads/2019/11/12 114400/UKROEd_eBook_English_28_July_2020.pdf

- Approved Driving Instructors National Joint Council: https://www.adinjc.org.uk/

- Attempts at the practical on-road driving test and the Hazard Perception Test and the risk of traffic crashes in young drivers: https://pubmed.ncbi.nlm.nih.gov/21972858/

- BRAKE – the road safety charity: https://www.brake.org.uk/

- Driving Instructors Association: https://www.driving.org/

- Driving Instructors Learning Environment:http://thedile.com/

- Driving test quotas:
  https://www.theguardian.com/uk/2005/mar/01/transport.world1

- Driving Test Success Theory Training:
  https://www.drivingtestsuccess.com/

- DVSA Practice your Theory: https://www.gov.uk/take-practice-theory-test

- DVSA Special Test DVSA special tests for instructors:
  https://www.gov.uk/dvsa-special-tests-for-instructors

- Engage Driving Scheme: https://engagedriving.co.uk/

- Federation of Small Businesses: https://www.fsb.org.uk/

- Guild of Experienced Motorists:
  https://www.motoringassist.com/the-gem-story/road-safety-charity/

- Honest Truth road safety scheme: https://thehonesttruth.co.uk/

- How to complain to the DVSA about your driving instructor:
  https://www.gov.uk/complain-about-a-driving-instructor

- How to report illegal driving instructors:
  https://www.gov.uk/report-an-illegal-driving-instructor

- IAM Advanced Driving Tests: https://www.iamroadsmart.com/

- Information on traffic cameras:
  https://www.rospa.com/media/documents/road-safety/speed-cameras-factsheet.pdf

- Institute of Master Tutors of Driving: https://www.imtd.org.uk/

- Liverpool Chamber of Commerce: https://www.liverpoolchamber.org.uk/

- Master drivers club with the DIA:
  https://advancedmotoring.co.uk/services/diamond-tests/

- More information on speed limits: Speed limits - GOV.UK (www.gov.uk)

- Motor Schools Association: https://msagb.com/

- New drivers losing their licenses:
  www.brake.org.uk/how-we-help/raising-awareness/our-current-projects/news-and-blogs/33-new-drivers-have-licences-revoked-every-day-in-2018

- Revenue collected in fines and penalties from driving offences:
  https://assets.publishing.service.gov.uk/government/uploads/system/uploads/attachment_data/file/648328/FOI2017-13509_-_Revenue_collected_in_fines_and_penalties_from_driving_offences.pdf

- Road Safety Research Report No. 81 Cohort II: A Study of Learner and New Drivers Volume 1:
  https://webarchive.nationalarchives.gov.uk/+/http://www.dft.gov.uk/pgr/roadsafety/research/rsrr/theme2/cohort2/cohrtiimainreport.pdf

- Roadcraft quiz: https://roadcraft.co.uk/roadcraft/roadcraft-quiz/

- Roadcraft the police driving manual: www.roadcraft.co.uk/

- Seat belt law: https://www.gov.uk/seat-belts-law

- St. Helen's and District Group of Advanced Motorists:
  https://www.iamroadsmart.com/groups/sthelensam

- The Association 4 Road Risk Management (ARM):
  https://www.arrm.org.uk/

- The Driving Instructor and Trainers Collective www.theditc.co.uk

- Theory Test Pro: https://www.theorytestpro.co.uk/

- Top 10 tips to stay within the speed limit:
  https://www.rospa.com/rospaweb/docs/advice-services/road-safety/drivers/top-ten-tips-for-staying-within-the-limit.pdf

- UKROEd - National Driver Offender Retraining Scheme:
  https://www.ukroed.org.uk/

- What happens to the body in a collision?
  https://rac.com.au/car-motoring/info/body-injuries-crash

- Young Enterprise: https://www.young-enterprise.org.uk/

Appendix 10

Recommended reading

- Who's in the driving seat by Ged and Claire Wilmot
- Standards Check Success: New revised edition for 2019 by Lynn Barrie
- Come to Coaching by Lynn Barrie
- The Motor Car Mechanical Principles by Dr John M Wells
- Roadcraft the Police Driver's Handbook
- The official DVSA Guide to Learning to Drive
- The Official Highway Code - every home should have one
- Can Drivers Really Teach Themselves? A Practitioner's Guide to Using Learner Centred and Coaching Approaches in Driver Education by Ian Edwards
- The official DVSA Driving the Essential Skills
- Driver Behaviour and Training by Dr Lisa Dorn
- Mind Driving: New Skills for Staying Alive on the Road by Stephen Hayley
- Coaching for Performance by Sir John Whitmore
- Driving instructor's handbook by John Miller
- How to become a driving instructor by Bill Lavender
- L of a way 2 Pass by Diane Hall

Appendix 11

UK Speed Limits	Built-up Areas**	Single carriageways	Dual carriageways	Motorways
Cars, motorcycles, car-derived vans and dual-purpose vehicles	30	60	70	70
Cars, motorcycles, car-derived vans and dual-purpose vehicles when towing caravans or trailers	30	50	60	60
Motorhomes or motor caravans (not more than 3.05 tonnes maximum unladen weight)	30	60	70	70
Motorhomes or motor caravans (more than 3.05 tonnes maximum unladen weight)	30	50	60	70
Buses, coaches and minibuses (not more than 12 metres overall length)	30	50	60	70
Buses, coaches and minibuses (more than 12 metres overall length)	30	50	60	60
Goods vehicles (not more than 7.5 tonnes maximum laden weight)	30	50	60	70 60 if articulated or towing a trailer
Goods vehicles (more than 7.5 tonnes maximum laden weight) in England and Wales	30	50	60	60
Goods vehicles (more than 7.5 tonnes maximum laden weight) in Scotland & NI	30	40	50	60

** A built-up area is any road (except motorways) with street lighting and no speed limit signs.

Handout available at https://insight2drive.co.uk/an-insight-to-drive-the-book/

Funny Stories

Finally, here are some funny stories of my own…

Halfway through a speed awareness course, one lady was quite agitated. She tapped the desk with her finger and said, "This is ridiculous, there should be a device in the car to tell you what speed you are doing." The room went silent, everybody turned towards her, stifling laughter.

I replied, "Yes there is a dial on your dashboard and all you've got to do is match the number on the dial to the number on the road sign." I am pleased to say she saw the funny side.

A lady on a driver awareness course, this is the course that was created especially for people who have had a collision, said, "I shouldn't be here on this course, I don't understand it, if the car wasn't parked there, I wouldn't have hit it, nobody ever parks there!"

One day when driving with a pupil, in light rain, the windscreen misted up. So, I said, "You can clear the windscreen, you know." So, the pupil dutifully took the back of her hand and wiped the inside of the windscreen with her hand. This taught me a valuable lesson, say what you mean, mean what you say. From that day onwards I say, "You can pop the wipers on, you know." I am sure the instructors I have trained are sick to death of me saying "Say what you mean, mean what you say!"

Another day I was taking a young chap on his driving lesson. While we were driving along, we were discussing anticipation skills. I was pointing out various things like the taxi in front might pull over, because I had seen the person inside lean forward. Sure enough, the taxi pulled over. Everything I was pointing out then happened. He then started having a slight panic attack, "I need to pull over, I need to pull over." I said, "Okay, let's find somewhere safe then. As we were pulling over, I said, "It looks like it's going to rain." The second I said this, the rain started. As soon as we pulled over, he raved at me, "It's you, it's you, you must be some sort of voodoo queen, everything you're saying is happening, you even commanded it to rain! Have you got a chicken head or something under my seat?" It took me ages to calm him down again.

I fondly remember an elderly lady who was on a driving development course because she'd had a collision. She was tiny, so tiny

I had to put a cushion on the seat for her so she could reach the pedals. Unfortunately, her driving was very substandard. When I told her it was time she thought about giving up her licence, as her driving had well fallen below standard. Her reply was, "Oh Kathy, I was hoping you would say that, because I've been thinking about giving my licence up anyway and getting myself a motorbike instead." Words failed me!

I was on a driving assessment with an elderly gent. We were on a 30mph speed limit road. He accelerated, going faster and faster. I told him it was a 30mph speed limit, he replied, "I know, I know. I'm trying to get up to 30." He pointed at the dial and said, "Look at the dial!"
He was looking at the rev counter; he was trying to get to 3000 revs!

On a driving test, in the days when I had a red Micra. My pupil went out into the car park with the examiner. I looked out of the window to watch them drive off. To my horror, my pupil and examiner walked towards a blue Corsa and tried to get into it. I rushed out to stop them, then pointed to my car. The learner driver, who had been driving my red Micra for about 30 hours, said "Oh, I didn't notice it was a red car!"

One lady driver once said that she was far happier *before* doing the education course she was on, because it is better to be oblivious to the facts and risks!

One driver asked me why the motorway chevrons are in rows of 99. I looked at her puzzled and she said "Well, you have to have something to do when driving at 70mph on a motorway."

A quote from a driving course. "I used to drive 100mph on the motorway, daily. I'm a much better driver when driving fast, if I drive too slowly, I look around and get distracted!"

I can't believe what someone said recently on a driving course, "Everyone drives 85mph along the A55 in North Wales". When questioned further, "Do you ever overtake anyone?" The answer was no! Next question "Does anyone overtake you?" Answer - still no! Are we the only ones who think this is bizarre?

During lockdown when delivering driving courses online I had one person who wanted to sit in bed while doing the course, another one wanted to ride an exercise bike, and someone else wanted to do it on their mobile phone while driving! Strange times indeed.

Thank you so much for reading, and I hope you enjoyed it and got the information you were looking for. Hopefully, we can eradicate bad practice and poor behaviour, not only within the driving instructor industry, but in driving as a whole.

Two of my favourite quotes
"There is no time to do everything, so just do the important things"
&
"If it is to be, it is up to me"

Kathy

Lightning Source UK Ltd.
Milton Keynes UK
UKHW012017261121
394655UK00003B/907